THE SHIPS THAT CAME
TO THE POOL OF
LONDON

THE SHIPS THAT CAME TO THE POOL OF LONDON

From Roman Galley To HMS *Belfast*

NICK ROBINS

AMBERLEY

Front Cover: Paddle steamer *Waverley* (1947) departing the Upper Pool on an excursion to the seaside. [Author]

The Brazilian officer training ship *Brasil* (1981) alongside the museum ship *Belfast* in September 2016. [Author]

Back Cover: The *Baltraffic* (1918) leaving the Upper Pool stern first while dragging her anchor to maintain the bows in central position in the channel beneath Tower Bridge.

First published 2017

Amberley Publishing
The Hill, Stroud
Gloucestershire, GL5 4EP

www.amberley-books.com

British Library Cataloguing in Publication Data.
A catalogue record for this book is available from the British Library.

ISBN 978 1 4456 6461 3 (print)
ISBN 978 1 4456 6462 0 (ebook)

Origination by Amberley Publishing.
Printed in Great Britain.

Contents

Preface

The Pool of London has long been a busy place. It has been the focus of seaborne trade with the city since the Roman galleys first arrived. It became home to the Hanseatic League, which recognised the strategic importance of London as a port and a trading centre. The river hosted a significant shipbuilding industry and the Pool also had a number of associated docks – St Katherine Dock, Shadwell Basin, and London Dock – which provided berths for the sailing clippers and later the steamers. Imposing warehouses were constructed to store goods, safe from both the weather and pilferers; several of these buildings survive to this day including Butler's Wharf and Hay's Wharf on the south bank of the Upper Pool. The Pool was split into the Upper and Lower Pool by the construction of Tower Bridge in the 1890s.

The sailing packets were followed by wooden-hulled paddle steamships while the deep sea fleets relied more on sail until the mid-nineteenth century. The Pool developed an important connection with Northern Europe and the near Continent, but as ships travelling further afield became larger, they migrated to the new dock systems downstream. Barges cluttered up the riverside wharves delivering and collecting goods from up and down river and transhipping cargoes from the docks and the numerous colliers bringing coal to the city from north-east England slowly discharged their cargo into lighters while lying in the river. In its heyday, the Pool was alive with the bustle and activity of trade, although little of this could be seen by the public other than the views available from London Bridge and Tower Bridge.

This is the story of the ships that came to the Pool and with it, the development of London as a port and an international commercial centre. It is a vibrant story, full of colour and excitement, complete with numerous Royal visits and nowadays regular arrivals of foreign cruise ships as well as naval ships of all kinds. It is a story that will appeal to a wide readership, including the many visitors that come to see HMS *Belfast*, as it describes the evolution of the shipping that used the Pool right up to the modern day trip boats and commuter services.

Nick Robins
Crowmarsh, February 2017

Chapter 1

The Pool of London

From Tower Pier to Shadwell the route lies through the historic Pool of London, past the Tower, under Tower Bridge, and then skirts the St Katherine and London Docks, mainly hidden by the riverside wharves. On the south bank is Bermondsey and a little further on is St Mary's Rotherhithe. At the end of the Lower Pool is the entrance lock to the London Docks adjacent to the Shadwell Memorial Park. Ahead is seen St Anne's, Limehouse...

What's What In Shipping: A Souvenir Guide to the River Thames
and to Places Served by Eagle Steamers
1963

Visitors to London have always been drawn to the river. Most know that the uppermost end of the Pool of London is London Bridge and many think that its lower end coincides with Tower Bridge. That belief defines just the Upper Pool, as the Pool continues downstream through the Lower Pool to Cuckold's Point Stairs, almost opposite the Canary Wharf development. The Upper Pool is just under 1 kilometre in length whereas the Lower Pool is a little over 3 kilometres long, so that the entire Pool occupies a 4 km stretch of the river. The lower end of the Pool was defined originally as a gravel spit protruding from the peninsular that ends at what is now Cuckold's Point Steps. At one time, the spit dammed up the water in the Pool at low tide to make a safe anchorage for small ships.

Cuckold's Point was named after a maypole with a pair of cuckold's horns on top, which was placed there in 1562 (a cuckold was traditionally represented with horns on his head). As a warning to all husbands, it probably had more to do with the Horn Fair, which was held at a permanent site nearby – although legend has it that King John granted a local estate to a miller whose wife he had allegedly seduced!

London Bridge was the only bridge across the river at London until 1729 when Putney Bridge was opened. The old London Bridge had the appearance of a Venetian-style bridge with houses and shops built along its sides. There were also waterwheels and other machinery slung below it to drive grinding stones to produce

An aerial view of the Pool of London situated between London Bridge and Cuckold Point with Tower Bridge separating the Upper Pool from the Lower Pool.

flour. The bridge stood for nearly 600 years, by which time the children's song 'London Bridge is falling down, falling down...' was first sung. The bridge was replaced in the early eighteenth century by a stone bridge that had graceful arches and which provided the main highway between the north and south banks of the Thames. It too was replaced when it started to subside into the soft underlying strata and again the children sang 'London Bridge is falling down...' The present wider stone bridge was opened by Her Majesty Queen Elizabeth II on 11 March 1973. The current bridge was built on a line some 30 metres upstream from its predecessors.

The first ships of any degree of sophistication to come into the Pool were the Roman galleys. These were tall vessels with a single square sail, some of considerable size; those engaged in the Egyptian grain trade displaced up to 400 tons. They were clumsy to handle and could only sail if the wind was well abaft the beam. A creek on the south bank of the river was a natural landing place and a large villa was built adjacent to it, served by a wooden landing stage. The Walbrook and Fleet streams on the north bank were also used to unload and load ships – there were no wharves as we know them today, only a few wooden jetties.

Tracey Bowman described the early history of London in her book on the Tower of London:

> The Romans had begun a settlement in London in AD 50, seven years after their invasion of Britain. It occupied a relatively small area… It was a well-drained and easily defensible site, overlooking marshy ground. The proximity of the River Thames made it easily accessible from the Continent, which aided commerce as well as communication. But just ten year after its founding, London was destroyed by Boudicea and her forces, who revolted against Roman rule in AD 60. It was quickly rebuilt on a larger scale, however, and from about AD 70 it became known as Londinium… The Roman historian Tacitus described the city as 'packed with traders'. By about AD 80 it also had a bridge across the Thames, close to the site of the present London Bridge.

Roman defences included a riverside wall and an enclosed compound around the site, later occupied by the Tower of London. In AD 410 the Romans were succeeded by invading Germanic tribes and the city went into decline. No ships approaching the size of the Roman galleys were seen in the Thames for many years after the dissolution of the Roman Empire. In due course the Vikings traded regularly to London, exchanging skins and fur for grain. In time, London became a valuable potential prize. Of course,

Viking traders in the Pool. [From an oil painting by nineteenth century Dutch artist Everhardus Koster]

The Great Fire of London 1666.

in autumn 1066, William, Duke of Normandy, invaded England and defeated King Harold at the Battle of Hastings; he took London from the south – having crossed the Thames at Wallingford, to the south of Oxford – and built two fortresses to suppress his unruly citizens. Work began on the Tower in the late 1070s within the eastern fortification, situated on the north bank of the Pool.

During the next ten years William (the Conqueror) built his White Tower – the Tower of London – as a symbol of his authority over the oppressed townsfolk. In 1147 Queen Matilda established St Katherine's church-cum-hospital immediately downstream of the White Tower. During the Middle Ages the adjacent boggy land was frequently inundated when the Thames wall was breached, but in the early sixteenth century the marshes were drained by Cornelius Vanderdelft, allowing waterfront development to begin.

For centuries, cargo vessels traded at riverside wharves in and around the City of London. As markets developed the quays became overcrowded and many boats took to mooring in midstream – unloading and loading their cargoes to and from barges. As early as 1586, William Camden – author of the seminal book *Britannia,* a survey of Britain – boasted of the Pool: 'A man would say, that seeth the shipping there, that it is, as it were, a very wood of trees disbranched to make glades and let in light, so shaded it is with masts and sails.'

The only time that the Pool of London fell silent, with no boats or ships to be seen, was in 1665 during the Plague. Sea coal from the Northumbrian coast was brought as far as Greenwich and Deptford and after the colliers had left, the lightermen would arrive to tranship it up-river. The following year was that of the Great Fire of London, which started in Pudding Lane and soon spread to the warehouses and stores along the north bank of the Pool. The fire was encouraged by the storage of such goods as brandy, pitch, resin and sulphur, all stored together, and the flames were fanned by a strong easterly wind. Rebuilding of the north bank wharves and stores was carried out under stricter regulations regarding party walls and the safe storage of combustible goods. Following such calamity, the Dutch took it upon themselves to invade the port, having blockaded the Thames Estuary for some time. After several attempts they were beaten off, leaving the business of the Port of London to get back to some semblance of normality.

The busy settlement that grew up at St Katherine's Hospital was destroyed by the St Katharine Docks Act, which was passed in 1825. Over 11,000 people were displaced by the works, which swept away slums at grim and aptly named places such as Dark Entry, Cat's Hole, and Pillory Lane. Construction of the new docks was led by the great railway builder Thomas Telford – his only major project in London. Some 2,500 men were employed to move rubble and soil (including the remains from the churchyard) into barges that were then taken up-river by the contractor Thomas Cubitt and used as foundation material for properties in Belgravia and Pimlico. Telford created the docks around two connected basins, giving an exceptionally long quayside for such a small area of enclosed water. Warehouses were erected on the docksides, with roadways running directly behind – an innovation designed to reduce handling and pilferage.

The new St Katharine Dock opened in October 1828 and the last of the warehouses was completed the following year. Additional warehousing was constructed in the 1850s. With its tight security, St Katharine Dock specialised in high-value exotic goods

St Katherine Dock *c.* 1880, from a contemporary print.

Hays News for autumn 1964 bringing news of a diverse range of interests to the employees within the Hays Group, to clients, and to other interested parties.

such as ivory, indigo powder, shells and feathers, as well as handling staples like tea and wool.

As Britain's empire expanded and the industrial revolution took hold, the Pool became the busiest section of river. It was crammed with ocean-going ships bearing exotic produce from foreign lands, but there was also skiffs bringing oysters and fish from the North Sea, and the sailing colliers with coal from north-east England.

At the end of the eighteenth century the very first police force was created in order to prevent theft and fraud taking place within the Pool of London. At the same time, imposing warehouses were constructed to store goods securely and safe from the weather. Several of these survive to this day, notably Butler's Wharf and Hays Wharf on the south bank of the Upper Pool.

The creek, which once had a Roman landing stage, later offered the same use to the Abbot of Battle, Sussex, who built his London home on the site of the Roman Villa. Slowly the creek became used as a tidal dock and is described as such in documents dating from 1501. R. H. Herbert in an article in *Hays News*, autumn 1964, described its subsequent development:

> ...it was not until around 1850 that the dock as we know it came into being when, as part of the construction of Hays Wharf Warehouses, the creek was diverted into a sewer and its old bed enlarged and enclosed and timber dock gates fitted at the entrance. The old creek, today wholly covered for the whole of its length, is used as a surface water sewer and can still be seen, particularly after heavy rains, where it discharges into the Thames at Battlebridge Stairs. This early dock was quite unmechanised; all cranes were hand operated requiring seven men to a crane. There was a hand capstan requiring 40 men and no catwalk around the edges of the dock; there was also no flood barrier and the water spilled over at high tide.

No sooner was the dock and associated warehouses completed when they were destroyed by fire, Herbert again:

> Within a few years of completion, the dock experienced the first real excitement in its life – the Tooley Street fire. It was low tide when the fire was discovered and the only water available to the Brigade for some hours was that enclosed within the dock and so great was the activity and the excitement and the rushing hither and thither that one fire engine slipped bodily into the dock itself! There were two sailing ships berthed there at the time but fortunately the tide rose sufficiently to warp them out before the fire, which commenced at Cottons Wharf and spread to Hay's dockside buildings.

During reconstruction hydraulic cranes and a hydraulic capstan were installed, driven by a pumping engine at Cotton's Wharf. In due course power was provided centrally by the Hydraulic Power Company. One problem that was never solved was that of the dock silting up; the solution adopted for many years was to send a tug into the dock on a falling tide with the dock gates open and set the tug to churn up the mud with its propeller so that the mud could discharge in suspension out into the river as the water level fell!

Stress was put on London Bridge as the lowest crossing point of the river as new docks were built lower down the river and the overall volume of traffic to the port increased. In order to try to alleviate this pinch point, a new ferry was commissioned to run between Tunnel Wharf (later known as Middleton's Wharf) at Wapping, and

The Lord Mayor of London opening the new steam ferry across the Thames at Wapping in November 1877. [*The Illustrated London News*]

The opening ceremony of Tower Bridge in 1894 – the structure dividing the Pool into the Upper Pool and Lower Pool.

Church Stairs at Rotherhithe. Two small barge-like steam paddle ferries, the *Jessie May* and the *Pearl*, were built locally to run the service, which was ceremoniously opened by the Lord Mayor of London in November 1877. It provided for horse-drawn vehicles as well as passengers. However, the ferry did not pay its way and was closed in 1886. Brunel's pedestrian tunnel that had been opened nearby in 1843 had long-since been converted for use as a railway tunnel; clearly a new bridge was needed – eventually, this was to be Tower Bridge.

It was not until 1894 that the Pool was formally split into the Upper Pool and Lower Pool with the completion and opening of Tower Bridge. The design of Tower Bridge was the result of a public competition in which there were fifty entries. The winner was architect Sir Horace Jones, and civil engineer Sir John Wolfe Barry was appointed to oversee the construction. Work started with the two massive piers sunk into the river bed, which needed to be strong enough to support the 10,000 tons of steel that formed the framework for the bridge, while the two towers are each 65 m (213 feet) tall and the bascules weigh 900 tons apiece. Construction took eight years with up to 400 men employed on the site at any one time. Tower Bridge was officially opened on 30 June 1894 by the Prince of Wales (later King Edward VII). *The Times*, 2 July 1894, reported:

> Under a cloudless sky and as part of a pageant, which delighted tens of thousands of people, the new Tower-bridge, which deserves to be reckoned among the greatest engineering triumphs of the Victorian age, was declared open for traffic by land and water by the Prince of Wales with every circumstance of pomp and splendour.

In 1885 an Act of Parliament decreed that a security tug be stationed at Tower Bridge for as long as there is a Tower Bridge. The tug was to be funded by the Corporation of the City of London to ensure the security of the central towers and was to carry a large placard amidships with the wording 'Tower Bridge Tug'. The Tower Bridge Tug was charged with assisting those that may need help in negotiating the channel between the towers in order to prevent collision damage to the bridge structure; a secondary role was to help those in peril in the tideway! The twin bridges at Waterloo also received an attendant safety tug for many years, but London Bridge never enjoyed such luxury.

Initially the tug *Aid*, built in 1877, was commissioned as the Tower Bridge Tug, but she failed to come to the aid of those in need more than once. The duty was then largely taken by the Gaselee family owned tugs: *Mosquito*, built in 1893, and *Wasp*, completed in 1890. Later the *Musca* of 1922 was often stationed at the buoy in the Pool and it fell to her also to act as Tower Bridge Tug for much of the period after the Second World War – a duty she shared with a second *Wasp*, built in 1939. Apart from ships and barges passing through Tower Bridge a main concern was that of ships leaving the St Katherine Dock entrance near the bridge, particularly on a flow tide when there was a lot of barge traffic around. The contract between the City of London and Gaselee & Son was finally terminated in the early 1960s when parts of the original Act were repealed.

With the construction of inland docks such as West India and East India, and later Royal Victoria and Royal Albert, the larger ships abandoned the Pool and St Katherine Dock. However, the Pool remained a hive of activity specialising in coasting and the North European trades until the decline of the traditional dock systems after the mid-twentieth century. Thereafter, limited traffic remained with the riverside quays until their closure in the Pool in the late 1960s and early 1970s. HMS *Belfast* took up a permanent riverside position as a museum ship in the Upper Pool in 1971 (Chapter 12).

The character of the Pool, even when it was at its busiest after the Second World War, is encapsulated in an illustrated article by Robert Kee about the Pool in the *Picture Post*, 3 December 1949:

> It is the heart of the greatest city of the world, the oldest part of London's port. For centuries the foreign ships and native barges have moved across its waters. For centuries the smell of cinnamon and coffee, paper, tallow and cloves has drifted through its winding streets. And in that time a strange peace has settled over water and streets alike.

Out on the water, in the middle of the Pool, it is all very simple. The river swirls quietly past the polite old tug in flat soft sheets of lead. On the shore a small boy fishes for driftwood, an old man turns his back and scratches on the beach for lumps of coal. A swan floats past, contemptuous. Tower Pier, Wapping Old Stairs, Execution Dock – the names slide through history rather than space. Ahead in the distance by Free Trade Wharf a barge, rowed by hand, comes slowly round the bend from Limehouse Reach. There is no sound but the small throb of a tug's engine emphasising the peace of the water and, from somewhere almost on the horizon of time, a soft continuous murmur like the hum of a distant planet full of bees. That is the noise of London. But it doesn't come from the heart of London, this is the heart of London: the peace of the water of the Pool.

But what of the ships themselves – the ships that so few now remember? There might be one of the United Baltic Corporation's big passenger and cargo steamers loading for Gdynia at Mark Brown's Wharf and on the opposite side of the river one of the Dutch Batavia Line steamers on her quick turnaround from Rotterdam. Also in the Upper Pool would be one or perhaps two of the General Steam Navigation Company's steamers, whose names were those of birds in English, some in Dutch and some also in French, reflecting the main trading sphere of that company. The Danish-flagged United Shipping Company would also be represented in the Upper Pool with ships discharging dairy products and chilled meat.

Below Tower Pier the Edinburgh boat – perhaps the *Royal Fusilier* or *Royal Archer* – would be alongside the Hermitage Steam Wharf ready for her evening departure back

The sophisticated cargo handling arrangement at Hermitage Steam Wharf, which allowed access from the hold of ships directly to any one of five storage floors and was leased by the London and Edinburgh Shipping Company.

to Leith, with the Carron Line boat for Grangemouth loading immediately upstream. Lower down the river the Dundee boat would be at the Dundee Wharf and the Aberdeen boat at the Aberdeen Wharf. On the north bank at the Free Trade Wharf, ships of the Tyne-Tees Steam Shipping Company – perhaps the *Richard Welford*, or one of her consorts – would be loading for Newcastle. In the Shadwell Basin the Powell Line or its successors, Powell, Bacon & Hough Lines, and later Coast Lines, might have a passenger and cargo steamer loading for Liverpool via selected South Coast ports, while a host of other vessels both large and small loaded and unloaded at riverside wharves or in the shelter of St Katherine Dock or the Wapping Basin and London Dock.

St Katherine Dock was host to a number of coastal services including the Clyde Shipping Company, which ran regular passenger and cargo liner services via Ireland to Glasgow, and the British & Irish Company, which had its popular twice-weekly service to Dublin. Wapping Basin was home to an important cargo liner service from the centre of London right to the centre of Paris for many years (Chapter 3).

At the heart of all the business activity, the unloading and loading, the storing and the distributing, the collection, the checking and the all-important paper work, was the dock worker. Stevedore, warehouseman, clerk, customs official, policeman, and all the supporting activity of transport on land and on river, made up the bustle of the Pool, and there are the characteristic streets of Wapping and Rotherhithe, the dockers' pubs – of which a few such as the 'Prospect of Whitby' still exist – and the characteristic lilt of the East London accent, all of which collectively defined the Pool. Altogether this evokes the memory of Charles Dickens, who wrote in his classic Victorian novel *Oliver Twist*:

> Near to that part of the Thames on which the church of Rotherhithe abuts, where the building on the banks are dirtiest, and the vessels on the river blackest with the dust of colliers, and the smoke of close-built, low-roofed houses, there exists at the present day, the filthiest, the strangest, the most extraordinary of the many localities that are hidden in London, wholly unknown by name to the great mass of its inhabitant. To reach this place, the visitor has to penetrate through a maze of close, narrow and muddy streets, thronged by the roughest and poorest of water-side people, and devoted to the traffic they may be supposed to occasion. The cheapest and least delicate provisions are heaped in the shops, the coarsest and commonest of wearing apparel dangle at the salesman's door, and stream from the house parapet and windows. Jostling with unemployed labourers of the lowest class, ballast-heavers, coal-whippers, brazen women, ragged children, and the very raff and refuse of the river…

The Pool, of course, was also the home of the popular excursion steamers that took Londoners away from the hustle and bustle and the grime of their city for a day out at the seaside. The ships were known by Londoners as the 'butterfly boats', as they only came out in the summer and then fluttered about! For years these were either tendered in mid-river or berthed at Fresh Wharf below London Bridge and at Charing Cross above it; in later years Tower Pier, now replaced by the Tower Millennium Pier,

The GSN 'butterfly boat' excursion ship *Crested Eagle* (1938) laid up for the winter at the GSN repair yard at Deptford in 1952, with the cargo ship *Woodcock* (1948) on the quay beyond.

Day trippers boarding the excursion steamer *Crested Eagle* (1925) at Tower Pier in the early 1930s. The GSN steamer *Leeuwarden* (1929) is at Brewer's Quay beyond; she was serving between London and Dutch ports.

became the home of the butterfly boats. I wrote in my *An Illustrated history of Thames Pleasure Steamers*:

> As Tannoy systems were introduced to the vessels the traditional live band was slowly replaced by the gramophone. Naturally, each ship adopted its own signature tune, and logically each time the *Laguna Belle* approached one of its piers strains of 'Lily of Laguna' would be heard across the water. The *Royal Eagle*, which was to be commissioned for the 1932 season, had an unfortunate habit of playing 'Open Up Dem Pearly Gates' each time she approached Tower Bridge, and of course 'La Marseillaise' was obligatory for any steamer whilst entering a French port.

Before all that, the Pool hosted the clipper ships in from the Great Tea Race of 1866 and of earlier years. It had hosted the brigs, schooners and other sailing craft that characterised the North Sea coastal trade, especially the numerous Geordie colliers. It was home to the West Indiamen and before them the heavy and clumsy sailing ships that sailed the world on voyages of discovery and developing trade. The East India Company's ships were generally of too a deep a draught to come up to the Pool and discharged at Blackwall, transhipping goods to sailing hoys or sailing barges for discharge in the city. Once upon a time, there were the Roman interests in the port and their ancient galleys of Phoenician origin, which also tied up in the Pool to work cargo.

Nowadays the Pool is still a natural focus, not least for visitors to London. The museum ship HMS *Belfast* is now permanently moored in the Upper Pool for visitors to enjoy and for them to remember the turbulent recent past that this light cruiser was designed to cope with. In the Lower Pool are a number of historic ships, the Thames barge *Will* lies at Hermitage, for example, while a host of other interesting artefacts are to be found on both sides of the river and within the old St Katherine Dock marina complex (Chapter 12). River cruises pass up and down and the fast commuter catamarans bring workers into the City and take them home at night, while also offering an ideal platform for sightseeing.

This is a far cry from the hustle and bustle of the Pool in the 1920s; the scene at Brewer's Quay, described by Cope Cornford in his centenary history of the General Steam Navigation Company, describes smells, noises, and action now long gone:

> At night, the steamships laden with meat, and the steamships bringing vegetables and fruit, draw alongside the wharf, and disgorge huge carcases of meat, which are piled into vans and carried to Smithfield in time for the early market, while the vegetables and fruit go to Covent Garden. The noise of strong hooves striking the ground, and the roll of wheels, reverberates in the arched tunnel leading from the wharf to the street, which is lighted below by an unearthly glare, and whose straight walls rise into the dark and are lost in wavering shadow. This is Port of London whence the people of London are fed. Here is but one wharf, at the miles of wharves at which the cargo boats of the British sea traders are loading and unloading, by day and by night, the year in and the year out...

The Pool may have changed immensely since the 1920s and its subsequent commercial demise brought about in the late 1960s by the onset of roll-on roll-off ferries and containerisation, but it is still the Pool. It is steeped in history, from the numerous Royal visits to the Blitz of the Second World War, but it remains, and always will remain, the Pool of London, complete with its Traitor's Gate, its bridges, wharves and docks, and all the other artefacts that remain for the visitor to enjoy.

Chapter 2

The Development of London as a Port

London is traditionally the administrative centre of England. London's river, the Thames, is navigable through the city and despite its fixed bridges still allows vessels, of low air draught, access to Twickenham and the non-tidal and regulated River Thames above it. It was natural, therefore, that the River Thames should become a focus for seaborne trade with northern Europe, the near Continent, and the Mediterranean region, and that it should also develop trade with the Far East and the Americas.

Well before the Romans arrived in Britain, London had become established as the lowest fording point of the River Thames. A gravel spit held back the water in what became known as the Pool and allowed access for people and carts between the north and south banks. The margins of the river were otherwise marshy and inhospitable and were certainly unsuitable for loading and unloading ships. As a consequence, hithes or wharfs were constructed at both Queenhithe and at Billingsgate so that trade with the Continent could begin and London could start to develop as a market and a focus for trading.

William the Conqueror recognised the strategic advantages of London. He bargained with its inhabitants and granted them their first Charter. During the period of the Conquest there was an influx of foreign merchants into London from Normandy, Flanders, Italy, Spain, and other European countries; the merchants perceived London as a suitable location for their trading purposes and they stocked with imported merchandise. The many Teutonic traders founded the Hanseatic League in the twelfth century, which was designed to bind the numerous German interests together for protection and commercial advancement, and the Hanseatic League exercised a powerful influence in Europe for several centuries. The League's headquarters were in London and they had a secure wharf at the Steelyard off Thames Street, near Blackfriars, where they were exempt from English jurisdiction. By the late sixteenth century English trade outweighed theirs and in 1598 Queen Elizabeth I closed the Steelyard and curbed the powers of the League.

The first Navigation Law was passed by Richard II in 1390 so that all imported and exported goods had to be carried in English ships. This fostered the shipbuilding

London as it appeared in the mid-thirteenth century.

The Steelyard near Blackfriars – the German merchant's wharf that was closed down by Queen Elizabeth in 1598. [From an undated Victorian engraving]

industry, which was then centred on the Thames, made ship owning more profitable, and widened the skills base of seafarers. The city fathers saw the potential of these activities for generating funds and increased their hold over the administration of the Port. In the reign of Edward IV, for example, the City Corporation obtained the right to weigh, measure and warehouse all wool brought to London, to pack woollen cloths, shins and all other goods, to examine all merchandise liable to Customs dues, to undertake porterage for foreign merchants, and to process all spices and to gauge wine.

In 1553 a foreign trade mission to Russia developed into the Russia Company, one of the most successful of the early maritime companies. The Turkey Company was established later and other similar merchant companies were formed under promises of monopolies to trade with specific countries. One of the most important of these for

Testing wine unloaded onto one of the Legal Quays above Brewer's Wharf. [From an old engraving]

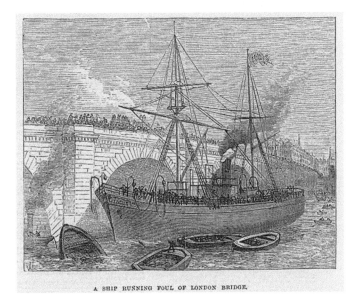

A SHIP RUNNING FOUL OF LONDON BRIDGE.

The second stone London Bridge completed in the early nineteenth century; an accident that happened more than once when the force of the tide was misjudged.

London was the formation of the East India Company. The Dutch had monopolised the trade with the Spice Islands and in 1599 they raised the price of pepper from 3s (shillings) a pound to 8s a pound. London merchants called a meeting under the chairmanship of the Lord Mayor. This led to Queen Elizabeth signing the Charter of the English East India Company on 31 December 1599, and a convoy of five vessels sailed for the East Indies early in the New Year. The convoy returned thirty months later with a huge cargo of pepper (pepper and other spices, it should be remembered, were essential at that time for curing and preserving meat). Ultimately the activities of the East India Company led to India being annexed within the British Empire.

This increase in trade eventually promoted the development of new port facilities. These were constructed below London Bridge, which was then a stone bridge that had been completed in 1209 at the upper end of the Pool. By 1558 there were twenty wharfs all situated in the Pool below London Bridge and upstream of the Tower of London. These quays were the Legal Quays, with a total length of 433 m (1,420 feet). However, the Legal Quays soon became inadequate for the burgeoning trade and 'sufferance wharves' were introduced downstream, although these wharves had restricted privileges.

Events abroad were to favour the enlargement of London's commerce. Antwerp had in the earlier part of the sixteenth century become the great emporium of Europe. The revolt of the people of the Low Countries against their Spanish invaders culminated in the sack of Antwerp by the Duke of Parma in 1576, and the city's supremacy was destroyed. London merchants and financiers took advantage of this opportunity to make London the new great commercial and financial centre. At the same time, the transhipment trades began to grow and these subsequently became the source of much wealth and prestige in London.

Three small ships – the *Susan Constant, Godspeed* and *Discovery* – sailed from Blackwall in 1606 for a London Company of Merchant Adventurers under the leadership of Captain John Smith. Captain Smith established and founded the State of Virginia as the highlight of this voyage.

On 3 June 1668, the *Nonsuch* and *Eaglet* left Gravesend to explore Hudson's Bay; only the *Nonsuch* survived and she returned the following year with a valuable cargo of furs. Charles II sealed the Charter of the Company on 2 May 1670, so beginning a long-standing and fruitful association between London and Canada.

The large wooden-walls of the East India Company anchored off Blackwall, their cargoes being discharged to the Legal Quays in the Pool via covered hoys or barges. In the mid-seventeenth century the East India Company – or John Company, as it had become known – constructed a small wet dock at Blackwall for fitting out its vessels; the first dock on the Thames to be fitted with gates. The dock was later incorporated into the Brunswick Dock, which in turn was absorbed by the East India Dock.

Shipbuilding began on the Thames in the time of Alfred the Great, who is credited with having a small dock constructed in which ships for defence could be built. Royal Dockyards were established at Deptford and Woolwich by Henry VIII and by the middle of the sixteenth century Deptford had become the principal naval shipbuilding yard and store in the Kingdom. The Deptford Dockyard eventually closed down after the launch of the *Druid* in 1869. The big wooden-walls of the John Company were nearly all built at Blackwall and, later on, fast clippers were built in the same yard for the tea trade and the Australian wool trade.

The shipbuilding industry on the Thames never really adapted to steam and iron; London could not compete with raw materials more easily available to yards in the north of England and in Scotland. Nevertheless, the best known of all the steamships built on the Thames was the *Great Eastern,* built at Millwall in 1858. The *Thunderer,* launched in 1912, was the last ship built on the Thames for the Royal Navy.

The plague of 1665 temporarily halted all trade with the port and the following year the Great Fire destroyed nearly all the wharves and warehouses. Despite these setbacks trade was quick to recover. Special taxes were levied in order to raise funds for rebuilding the wharves, even though most of them were in shallow water that dried out at low tide. Royal Assent was given in 1696 to an enabling Bill for the construction of a wet dock at Rotherhithe; this dock was intended for fitting-out new ships, although in due course it was used for cargo handling.

Trade blossomed in the eighteenth century. Between 1700 and 1770 imports and exports doubled and between 1770 and 1795 they doubled again. London now handled nearly sixty-five per cent of all trade with England. The greatest increase in imported goods was sugar, rum, dyewoods, ginger, and pimento from the West Indies. While trade was buoyant, congestion in the river had become severe; up to 1,775 vessels were allowed into the Upper Pool at any time – an area intended to handle just 550 vessels – although all the ships were smaller than 500 tons gross. There were also more than 3,000 lighters then working in the river. Navigation was difficult and hazardous with barges manoeuvring with the tide, with one man aft to steer with a large oar. Goods often lay in open lighters awaiting discharge and pilfering was rife, while damage from the weather was not uncommon. Nevertheless, the wharf owners resisted all attempts to build new dock facilities that would ease the congestion as they believed that such a move would erode their own business.

In 1796 a Parliamentary Committee of the House of Commons was 'appointed to enquire into the best mode of providing sufficient accommodation for the increased trade and shipping of the Port'. The Committee, however, was unable to make any viable recommendations for improving matters and it was not until 1799 that Parliament passed a Bill for the construction of a dock on the Isle of Dogs 'for better regulating the Port of London', and in particular to ensure that 'West India produce might be effectually secure from loss by theft or other causes, and the public revenue greatly benefited'. The Bill was promoted by the West India Merchants in conjunction with the Corporation of London. The West India Company was granted a monopoly for twenty-one years to unload all West India produce brought into the Port and all exports to the West Indies were also required to be loaded in the new West India Dock. High walls and a wide ditch surrounded the West India Dock and an armed watch of 100 men and officers, each equipped with muskets, swords and pistols, plus 100 special constables, were employed to protect it. The dock was opened by the prime minister, Henry Addington, on 22 August 1802. The Free Water Clause, associated with the West India Dock Bill, gave wharfingers and lightermen the right to send barges into the docks without payment of dues. This was a critically important clause as it was only later realised that it allowed shipping companies a means of loading and unloading in the docks without payment of dock dues.

The Corporation of London obtained powers to construct a canal from Limehouse Reach to Blackwall Reach to save vessels navigating the hazardous and crowded bends in the river around the Isle of Dogs. The City Canal was opened in 1805, but it was little-used and was later bought by the West India Docks Company in 1829 and transformed into a timber dock.

The traditional cargo handling of ships lying in the river and loading and unloading into barges paid little heed to security, as Moyse-Bartlett described in his book on the history of the Merchant Navy:

> …it was not until the beginning of the nineteenth century that the crowded state of the River Thames forced the provision of suitable accommodation for the loading and discharging of vessels. At this time the larger vessels had to lie in the stream between Deptford and Blackwall; smaller ships could take their cargoes as far up as London Bridge. Sometimes well over a thousand vessels lay moored in the river together; offering a happy hunting ground for thieves of all description – 'light horsemen' collecting their booty at dead of night; 'river pirates', looting the barges and tenders, of which many hundreds lay moored together during the night-hours, inadequately watched, if at all; the 'mudlarks', hunting in the slime at low tide for the articles dropped overboard by their confederates among the stevedores; and the 'scuffle hunters' themselves, who hid their trophy about their persons until they could convey it ashore.

The Port facilities developed rapidly. Docks at Wapping were under construction before the West India Dock was opened, the London Dock Bill receiving the Royal Assent on 20 June 1800, and London Dock was opened in 1805. The London Dock had a twenty-one-year monopoly to receive all vessels entering the Port with tobacco, rice, wine and brandy (except from the East and West Indies). The warehouses included a large bonded warehouse that could accommodate 24,000 hogsheads of tobacco. War with France at this time had an adverse effect on the port as a whole, but all the new facilities were long overdue and were soon put to good use. Another enclosed dock – the East India Dock – opened in 1806. All ships arriving from the East Indies and China were required to load and unload here, and all these new docks were on the north bank of the river.

On the south bank at Rotherhithe (a hythe was a timber jetty), the old wet dock used as a fitting out basin was converted for extracting sperm oil from blubber brought in by whaling fleets, and its name was changed to the Greenland Dock. This did not last long and the dock was next used for the North European trade in timber, tar, and corn. St Katharine Dock opened in 1828 just below the Tower of London. The complex had two connected basins, the east dock and the west dock, which were linked to the river through an entrance lock 55 m (180 feet) in length and fitted with three pairs of gates. The lock was designed to handle either one large or two small ships. Two steam engines, designed by James Watt, pumped water up to the dock to maintain its level 4 feet above that of the river. Other docks were subsequently built on the south bank and all eventually passed to the proprietorship of the Surrey Commercial Docks Company.

The steamship made its first appearance on the Thames in 1815, with an erratic passenger service offered between Wapping Old Stairs and Milton, just beyond Gravesend (Chapter 5). Little by little the steamer started to erode sail and London soon became a significant hub for the domestic coasting trade. The smoky wooden paddle steamer first invaded the coastal schooner trades to East Anglia, Lynn, Hull, and beyond to Newcastle, Leith, Dundee and Aberdeen. By 1875 sail had become subordinate to steam in all trades, with port dues representing 5.1 million tons of goods by steamer and only 3.6 million tons by sailing ship.

Although the length of quays available was now able to service demand, the access to wharves and quays as well as the new docks was poor. The depth of the river channel was inadequate and there was no regulation of traffic. The large body of watermen and lightermen resented the introduction of steam tugs and steam passenger boats into the Port and used every device to obstruct them. These issues were finally addressed by the Thames Conservancy Act of 1857 which 'vested in the Conservators all title and rights in the bed, soil and foreshore of the river from Staines to Yantlet Creek and empowered them to carry out all conservancy duties, including the proper regulation of river traffic and the maintenance of the navigation channel'.

P&O's wooden-hulled paddle steamer *Euxene* (1847), alongside in one of the new docks at London.

The GSN steamer *Hirondelle* (1890) was the first of the fast long-distance steamers in the fleet and served on the prestigious London to Bordeaux route.

Dock construction continued apace. The West India Dock Company and the East India Dock Company amalgamated and the London and St Katharine Dock companies also combined. In 1874, the London & St Katharine Docks Company decided to construct the Royal Albert Dock as an extension of the Victoria Dock, which was opened in 1880 and at the time was the largest and finest dock in the world at 3 km long with 5 km of new deep-water quays. The dock eroded business from the East & West India Docks Company, which responded by building Tilbury Dock, some 10 km down-river from the City. This dock opened in 1886 but shipping was slow to transfer from the older docks, largely because of boycotts by the merchants, lightermen, and wharfingers. Business did eventually improve as shippers realised the benefits of the down-river facilities, which provided easy access to the sea.

Bonded warehouses had been introduced in 1803 as a privilege vested only with the dock companies. At the end of the monopolies initially granted to these companies, the bonding facilities were also extended to the riverside wharf and warehouse proprietors. The Dock companies began to feel the full effect of the privileges accorded to the lightermen in all dock legislation – the Free Water Clause, which enable barges to enter and leave the docks without payment of dues. By 1887 the London & St Katharine Docks Company (which also owned the Royal Victoria and Royal Albert Docks) and the East & West India Docks Company (which had built the Tilbury Dock) were in such a parlous financial state that they were forced to agree on a new working arrangement. As a consequence, the London and India Docks Joint Committee was given the management of all these docks in 1888. The joint committee took over the day-to-day management, but the capital of the two companies was not merged and the profits were distributed separately.

The significant increase in the size and draught of ocean-going ships required new facilities towards the late nineteenth century. However, the continued dispersion of powers among several authorities and companies prevented any work from being carried out. The government eventually sponsored a Royal Commission to inquire into the poor state of finances of the various dock companies and their inability to develop new facilities. The Commission sat for two years and, in June 1902, issued recommendations for the creation of a central authority; it was not until 1908 that the Port of London Act was passed. The President of the Board of Trade, Mr Lloyd George, arranged for £22.4 million to be made available for the purchase of the London & India Docks Company, Millwall Dock Company, Surrey Commercial Docks Company, and the river interests of the Watermen's Company. These were all vested with the newly empowered Port of London Authority, along with the management of the river below Teddington.

The primary duty of the Port of London Authority was 'to take into consideration the state of the river and the accommodation and facilities afforded in the Port and... to take such steps as they may consider necessary for the improvement thereof'. The Authority was entrusted with making good any deficiencies in the Port and of the equipment and services provided for both ships and goods. It also had to carry out all conservancy duties over the 110 km length of the tidal River Thames and exercise the powers previously vested in the Watermen's Company relative to the registration and licensing of craft and boats, as well as the lightermen and watermen themselves.

The riverside wharves, such as those within the Pool, remained outside the Authority's jurisdiction, and continued to trade independently. The proprietors of the private wharves and warehouses also continued to enjoy the advantages, directly and indirectly, of the privileges of the free use of the docks by barges.

Under the Port of London Authority's administration, a new dock facility – the King George V Dock – was opened in 1921 to complete the Royal Docks complex. The planning and initial construction of the King George V Dock began in the 1900s but construction was delayed by the First World War. The dock was designed to provide capacity for ships up to 30,000 tons gross, and represented the latest in dock planning and design. Construction of the dock cost over £4 million, and the entrance lock was big enough to accommodate the 35,655-ton Cunard liner *Mauretania* when she was commissioned in 1939. The Port of London Authority reserved marshland to the north, which is now Beckton, for further expansion of the dock system to create a fourth dock, but this was never built.

The busy King George V Dock and the departure of Glen Line's *Glengyle* (1939) 4 July 1961 for the Far East. From left to right, Union-Castle Line *Rhodesia Castle* (1951), P&O *Cathay* (1957), P&O *Singapore* (1951), and Cunard Line *Arabia* (1947). [Dr David Mason]

A crowded and busy scene: Brewer's Wharf in the Upper Pool in 1924. [From a sketch by W. L. Wyllie]

The Royal Victoria Dock was extensively rebuilt between 1935 and 1944 including the construction in 1937 of the new North Quay that replaced the five finger-jetties of the original Victoria Dock. The new quay was south of the original dock edge and new transit sheds were erected on the resulting reclaimed land during the early 1940s. The most important cargo was grain and the heavy investment in the 1930s resulted in the older Victorian granaries and mills being replaced by much bigger concrete structures.

Throughout all this expansion and development, the business to and from the Pool of London continued apace and was not in any way eroded by the development of the London Dock system. On the contrary, there was a synergy between the deep sea trades working from the dock systems and the North European and Continental trades, which had focussed on the former Legal Quays in the Pool. The Pool of London, however, had been the original focus of London's seaborne trade and was the original nucleus for the development of the Port of London.

London, like Liverpool, is a port favoured by a natural deep water approach. Both ports prospered as ships became larger in the nineteenth and twentieth centuries at the expense of ports with shallower approach channels. London further benefitted from its aspect with the Thames estuary – a focus for traffic to and from the Rhine and the Seine so promoting trade with the near continent. Both London and Liverpool were major *entrepôt* centres, providing employment and wealth throughout their respective hinterlands. They were also great transhipment ports, providing added value to the port itself; not surprising then that the two ports vied with each other for trade from the 1850s for well over the next 100 years.

New Fresh Wharf was a modern facility in the Upper Pool for working fruit. Note the transit sheds at quay level for sorting goods preparatory to dispatch to warehouse or to market, with the Belgian fruit carrier *Alfonso* (1950) unloading in the early 1960s.

Chapter 3

Trade in the Pool – And the Diplomatic Bag

I walked across London Bridge firmly resolved not to linger there. When I was almost at the Southwark end I saw a great crowd of boys and men leaning over the bridge, gazing downward towards the river in dead silence. Of course, I had to edge my way in; and what do you think I saw? I saw a foreign ship leaving London. The captain was on the bridge, the ship was edging its way gingerly into the river, and one or two of the deck hands, seeing the fringe of heads above on the bridge, cheerily waved to us. I am sure that not one of us did not wish he could sail away with that ship!

From H. V. Morton, *In Search of London*
1951

An indication of the early trade of the port is given by the list of tolls applied at Billingsgate, which was the first of the wooden hythes to be constructed. The tolls were applied under instruction from Ethelred at the end of the tenth century. For a ship with timber, one log was taken as toll. Small vessels with fish paid a half penny and larger vessels one penny. Rouen vessels with wine or dried fish paid six sous and five per cent of the fish. Vessels from Poitou, Normandy, and France showed their goods and went toll free. From Huy, Liege, and Nivelle, they paid the usual tolls.

Sir Joseph Guinness Broodbank, in his book *History of the Port of London*, wrote:

In 1306 we have the first mention of coal in connection with the Port of London. It appears in a grant of Edward I, made in the year authorising the citizens to levy imposts for the repair and maintenance of London Bridge, amongst which was a toll of 6d upon every cargo of sea coal passing under the bridge for the next three years. The coal was brought up the River Fleet and sold in the adjoining lane, now called Sea Coal Lane. Two years later we learn of complaints of the contamination of the atmosphere by smoke, leading to edicts ordering the use of coal to cease...

The year 1315 marks the record of the first trading ship belonging to a citizen and merchant of London – this was the *Little Edward*, owned and commanded by John Band, and working for the most part for the Hanseatic League out of London to Antwerp and other North Sea ports.

The earliest known map of London is Wyngaerde's panorama, dating from between 1543 and 1550. It is a panoramic view of the city and shows a large number of sailing vessels moored in the river. More than forty small vessels may be counted above London Bridge, but more than seventy big ships lie below the bridge. Of particular interest are seven spritsail topmast vessels lying off the Steelyard headquarters of the Hanseatic League. The image demonstrates that sophisticated sailing ships were trading to London at that time, Geoffrey Callender wrote in *Mariner's Mirror*, Volume 2, Part 7, for 1912:

> To what nationality these seven ships belonged it is impossible to say. The date of Wyngaerde's Map almost exactly synchronizes with a landmark in British Commercial History. For about this time the Merchant Adventurers were challenging in London the long-established supremacy of the Hanseatic League. Little, however, was really accomplished at the death of Edward VI and Mary's infatuation for Spain and Philip set the merchants of Antwerp on their legs again. Certainly, when Wyngaerde drew his map he did not forget to give due prominence to the Steelyard, the Hansards' headquarters. In those days it occupied the site which today is covered by Cannon Street Station. So perhaps these ships are vessels of the Hanse which from the beginning of the fourteenth century until the reign of Elizabeth brought to this country the wares of Russia, Hungary, Bohemia, Flanders, Brabant, Germany and France, 'jewels, silver bullion, quicksilver, wrought silks, gold and silver thread, camlets, grograms, glass, wax, salt, fur, timber, sugar, cotton, amber, cummin, linen fine and coarse, serges, tapestry, madder, hops, arms and ammunition, household furniture and other merceries of all sorts'.

The Hanseatic League supervised imports of ropes, masts, pitch, flax, hemp, linen cloth, wax, and iron. In return lead, tin, fish, meat, fat cattle and fine wool went back on the return voyage.

Fresh Wharf beneath London Bridge held the important function of discharging the fishing boats working in the Thames Estuary and beyond. The adjacent fish market ultimately developed into the wholesale Billingsgate Fish Market, still active today but in new premises, and the old market building remains an attractive landmark below London Bridge. The role of dealing with the fishing boats was carried out throughout medieval times, until the wharf later adopted the role of importing fruit from the Continent, the fishing trade having then focussed on Lowestoft and Margate.

As the great sea explorers slowly opened up trade with the wider world, so the trade of London developed – not least under the reign of Elizabeth I. Guinness Broodbank again:

> It is in this era that we find shipping anchoring below the City limits. Thus in 1513 we read of Deptford as a royal station for ships. The mention of Brook Street, Ratcliff,

Fishing boats at Billingsgate (Fresh Wharf). [From an engraving by E. W. Cooke 1929]

Landing oranges at Fresh Wharf, London Bridge 1874. [*The Illustrated London News*]

and of North Street, Poplar, in 1550, indicates that ships were moored in the river at these neighbourhoods. It is clear that the East India Company soon made Blackwall the headquarters for their shipping for we find that in 1612 a dwelling house and offices were built there...

For centuries, most of London's trade took place along the north bank of the Upper Pool, where the City met the Thames. Hay's Wharf was founded on the south bank in 1651 by Alexander Hay around a tidal creek. It was the oldest and the most successful of all London's general wharves and ultimately absorbed almost every other wharf on the south bank between London Bridge and Tower Bridge. It was known as the 'larder of London' because of its enormous trade in foodstuffs, mainly dairy and meat products, as well as tea and coffee. Up to three-quarters of all London's imported food passed through these wharves and through Hay's Dock, which was built along the line of the original creek. The first Custom House was built on the north bank in 1275: one of its most famous officials was Geoffrey Chaucer (1342-1400), author of *The Canterbury Tales*.

The early trade focussed on the north bank of what is now the Upper Pool and was essentially domestic. Arriving at the port were two basic commodities: food and fuel. Grain and other essential foodstuffs were brought by sailing brigs from south and east coast ports in order to feed the city; timber and later also coal were sourced from north-east England – the former both as a building material and as a fuel. The grain trade focussed on Irongate Wharf, the trade being first recorded there in 1758; the wharf was situated immediately downstream from the Custom House. Irongate Wharf much later became one of the homes of the London-based General Steam Navigation Company.

The coal trade was enormous. It started with the import to London of sea coal washed up on the shores of Northumberland and Durham, sourced by exposed coal

Imports at Customs House Quay from France 1757. [From an engraving by Louis Peter Boitard]

The Ellerman Lines' *Belgravian* (1937) lying alongside Butlers Wharf. She was sunk by torpedo in August 1941.

seams on the sea bed. By the late nineteenth century it had developed into a wholesale industry sponsored by the coal mine owners in north-east England. In the year 1808, for example, 15,913 ships are recorded to have moored in mid-river in the Pool, and by 1824 this had increased to 15,913; nearly all these entries were colliers. In 1824 a further 7,705 vessels were accommodated in the docks and at riverside wharves and hythes; the colliers, therefore, amounted to two thirds of the ship arrivals that year.

Overseas trade later migrated to the new dock systems downstream from the Pool. London Dock, however, remained the focus of some overseas trades as Captain J. Findlay recalled from the 1890s in an article in *Sea Breezes*, October 1949:

> There were very few steamers which occupied the London Dock at this time. Those of Messrs John Hall & Company, trading to ports in southern Spain in the wine and fruit trade, generally berthed at Shadwell Basin. Steamers of the Aberdeen Direct Line, better known perhaps as the Rennie Line, running to Natal and East African ports, always discharged and loaded at the jetty, London Dock. Smart looking packets with yacht-like appearance, hulls of French grey, yellow funnels, raked masts and square rigged on the fore, they all had African names, such as *Matabele, Insiszwa, Inkosi, Inyate…, Inchanga*, she had a fine saloon, all marble. All these steamers carried First Class passengers and ran a fortnightly service.
>
> Rennie's sailing ships were all small barques carrying about 800 tons, fitted out to carry passengers. Their loaded draught was 13 feet, so as to enable them to cross the bar at Natal [Durban]. They usually proceeded to Mauritius or India to load for home.

Morocco Wharf was so named, of course, because of its original use for trading to Morocco. It was the home of the Royal Mail Line steamers trading to Casablanca and other North African ports throughout the late Victorian era, bringing home exotic fruits and other goods in return for manufactured goods. Butlers Wharf, below Tower Pier, became the home of the Mediterranean traders belonging to GSN, Ellerman & Papyanni Lines and MacAndrews & Company, again bringing in a range of agricultural produce, fruits, wines and other goods. However, this was small beer compared with the near European trades then working out of the Pool, after much of the deep sea trade had migrated down-river to the better-equipped deep water docks. Most of GSN's non-Mediterranean traffic berthed above Tower Bridge.

Once the colliers had been ousted from the Pool (see Chapter 4), an ever-increasing pageant of steam cargo ships came and went to the riverside wharves and docks. These were essentially cargo liners running alongside the passenger and cargo liners on the domestic and European routes (Chapters 6 to 8). The new types of ships were of all sizes. They derived from a large and diverse number of British and European ship owners and ranged from the regular callers – both cargo and cargo/passenger steamers – to the chartered cargo ships charged with a specific cargo to or from London, many with no booked return shipment. Many of these ships docked in London Dock or Shadwell Basin rather than the riverside wharves and came and went much less publically than the ships on the regular liner services using the riverside wharves. What cannot be overstated was the continual activity – the smells, the noises, the general hustle and

A press photo taken in early October 1939, after war had been declared, is captioned 'Steamer combines the duties of long stop behind the wicket and sight screen for the bowler during a juvenile cricket match on Tower Beach, London, at low tide'. The steamer is GSN's *Groningen* (1928). [Acme Newspictures, New York]

bustle, both on the water and on the adjacent wharves and quaysides as well as the roads and lanes leading down to the river. Little of this was apparent to the Londoner other than the action to be seen from either London Bridge or Tower Bridge as they crossed the river on the way to work. Nevertheless, it was action that went on night and day.

The colliers were not completely removed from sight as coal still needed to come into the Pool and to destinations above London Bridge. For this, the low-lying 'flat-iron' type collier was developed, capable of negotiating up-river bridges merely by lowering masts and funnel, which were hinged for the purpose (Chapter 11).

The plethora of cargo ships that discharged and loaded in the Pool over the years carried an incredible aggregate cargo manifest. Tramp steamers were not often seen in the Pool as their staple cargoes were generally bulk commodities such as grain, ore or coal. However, tramp ships and relatively small cargo ships on the charter market were used to support the cargo liner trades from time to time. It was not uncommon to see Dutch coasters of all types and sizes in the Pool working on the Continental routes, while larger tramp steamers were occasionally used to uplift larger cargoes. The Danish dairy trade and the Mediterranean fruit business were too specialised for chartering and dedicated company-owned vessels were always used; fruit being carefully stowed with airways between each stack of boxes to allow ventilation of the cargo.

The outbreak of the First World War brought complete confusion to the dock and shipping industries. The government requisitioned materials, ships, road and rail transport, and diverted labour to other needs. Overall, however, trade continued as usual, although essentials, and not luxuries, were predominant. In fact, with Antwerp and Rotterdam out of use, the port initially benefited. The war was conducted mostly without air attack by either side, the only impact being that of the German U-boat campaign in 1917, which successfully discouraged shipping from using London for fear of attack and briefly interrupting trade. Hence, the port experienced minimal damage during these years and by the end of the war it was relatively easy for it to return to its continuing commercial development, despite the onset of the Depression in the late 1920s.

During the inter-war period the small passenger and cargo liners eventually became subordinate to cargo only ships. This was a response to falling passenger numbers due first to cheap rail fares offered in competition with the domestic routes and later the transfer of continental passengers to fast rail and ferry connections to many European cities. By the close of the Second World War, for example, there were few surviving European and domestic passenger and cargo liners and many were not in a state worthy of renovation to make them fit the trade. At that stage up to twelve berths were offered on some of the European routes, declining to less by the late 1950s, and few passengers now embarked or disembarked in the Pools. However, the Upper and Lower Pools were still extremely busy with ships often queuing for berths waiting patiently at the mid-river buoys.

One very important regular inter-capital cargo liner service emerged at the turn of the twentieth century. It was carried on out of sight from the London commuters crossing the Thames bridges, so it never attracted the glamour attached to the more visible services such as those to Poland and Spain. Barry Luthwaite reported in *Sea Breezes*, September 1973:

> The Compagnie Maritime de la Seine was founded towards the end of the last century [nineteenth] and after a transitional period as a ship-brokering and chartering agency handling cargoes passing through Rouen and Paris, commenced ship owning in 1899 with the prime intention of being able to offer shippers a new and regular service between Paris and London via Rouen. This link between the two ports lasted almost 70 years until sale of the final vessel operating the service in 1970.

The agent appointed in London was G. T. Symons & Company, and a berth was arranged at the Colonial Wharf in the Lower Pool at Wapping on the North Bank. Five new steamers were ordered from builders in Nantes: *Anjou, Artois, Aunis, Bearn,* and *Maine.* Each ship had an open bridge and the funnel, foremast, and mainmast could be lowered on hinges in order to pass under the numerous bridges on approach to Gennevilliers Quay at Paris. The steamer *Mabel* was also purchased from J. Burnett & Sons in order to remove her from her existing but irregular run between Cotton's Wharf in the Upper Pool and Paris. There had been a number of direct services to Paris over the years but none became as established as the new CMS service; this was a huge success, and at any time a spare steamer could be gainfully employed in the Mediterranean trades. During the First First World War a new ship was added to the service to replace vessels that had been sold. Navigation in confined waters at both ends of the trip resulted in a number of collisions in the Thames and at least one stranding in the Seine.

In 1923, Wm H. Muller formed a new British subsidiary to cream off some of the cross-Channel business. One link it adopted in earnest was in competition with CMS running between the Thames and Quai d'Austerlitz at Paris. Just before the appointed sailing hour a car from the Foreign Office would deliver the diplomatic bag to the British-registered ship loading at Wapping Basin, London Dock, to take to the Embassy in Paris, just as the French delivered their diplomatic bag to the master of the CMS ship on departure from Paris! Business was good and throughout the remainder of the interwar years and post-Second World War there was room for both companies to ply on the same inter-capital City route out of the Pool – a situation that remained unchanged until 1970.

Three new motor ships replaced the old steamers from 1933: *Gatinais*, *Nivernais*, and *Dijonnais*. Only the *Nivernais* survived the Second World War, during which the ships were used elsewhere. Replacements were the new *Gatinais* and *Dijonnais*, which were ordered in 1949. A fourth ship, the *President E Chalas*, joined the fleet in 1958. In 1962 the company moved from Colonial Wharf downstream to Woolwich and then three things happened in quick succession: first, a merger with the Muller line service to Paris; second, a retrenchment to the Muller's St George's Wharf at Rotherhithe; and, finally, CMS decided to withdraw from the service altogether and sold its interests and ships to G. T. Symons, its London agent.

Wm H. Muller's regular thrice-weekly direct service to Paris from Wapping Basin in London Dock was operated by the *Meuse*, *Scheldt*, and *Somme*, all still British-registered. They were of low air draft; the highest point of the *Seine*, for example, was the top spoke of the ship's wheel, enabling her to negotiate the fourteen fixed bridges up to the berth at Quai d'Austerlitz in central Paris. But times were changing and it was not long before the joint service also came to an end; in 1970, the route was wound up and closed. Thus, in a short period of time, the three sailings a week service was reduced first to one sailing and then terminated by the joint operators, Muller and G. T. Symons as successors to CMS, on a longstanding and successful route. Yet again the onset of vehicle ferries and containers had proved the better of traditional break bulk cargo handling methods, while the diplomatic bag now travels under the Channel by Eurostar.

A boost to the deep sea traffic in the Pool was made in the height of the 1930s depression when New Fresh Wharf was opened. This stretched almost from London Bridge to Adelaide House on the north bank, and encompassed the old Fresh Wharf and all of Cox and Hammonds Wharf. It offered state-of-the-art cargo handling facilities, including chilled and refrigerated storage facilities on five floors. New Fresh Wharf was also at the heart of the city and adjacent to its specialist wholesale markets.

New Fresh Wharf could accommodate ships up to 10,000 tons gross – the largest ships then able to enter the Upper Pool. From the outset it attracted Vestey's Blue Star Line interests, which started bringing big ships up to New Fresh Wharf to discharge fruit initially from South American ports and, from 1934 onwards, also from Australia and New Zealand. It was not uncommon to see large cargo liners discharging just below London Bridge in the 1930s and a variety of owners sent vessels up-river to this facility before they returned to the docks to load for their outward journey. For example, the *Celtic Star* and her fleet mates were a familiar sight below London Bridge. Even in the 1960s, the *Canadian Star* made at least one visit and ships such as the Greek reefer *Sifnos* came up to the Pool several times. Once again cargoes were arriving in the Pool from all five continents and the Upper Pool had truly become an international centre for traffic once more.

The Blue Star Line's *Celtic Star* (1918) working frozen goods from Argentina at New Fresh Wharf in the Upper Pool in 1934.

The Greek refrigerated ship *Sifnos* (1962) discharging at Fresh Wharf; she belonged to the Reefer & General Shipping Company of Piraeus.

Fires in St Katherine Dock and the Lower Pool at the height of the blitz in 1941.

With the outbreak of war on 2 September 1939 the Royal Navy established guard ships, while batteries were manned on both banks of the lower river. Barrage balloons were inflated in the middle of the reaches in the dockland areas and in industrial areas. Everyone was aware that at some point the Thames would become a target and defences in the Port were prepared amid strict security of the dock estates. The port passed into the control of Port Emergency Committees responsible to the Ministry of Transport; the London Committee consisted of existing members of the Port of London Authority, but with broader responsibilities and powers.

During November 1939 the Luftwaffe first targeted the Thames Estuary and throughout the war this area was heavily bombed. The first significant air attack on London was on 7 September 1940 when 375 enemy planes dropped bombs over the docks and the East End in particular. For fifty-seven consecutive nights the tideway was under almost continuous attack with transport, communication systems, sheds and warehouses destroyed or damaged, including much of the warehouse storage at St Katherine Dock, which was never rebuilt. The main dock system fared better and offered business as usual during 1941.

It was during this period that the river came into its own, being used as the main City highway. A service of tugs and launches was provided by the Port Emergency Committee on behalf of the London Passenger Transport Board and regular passenger timetables were established.

Nevertheless, by the end of 1941 shipping traffic in the Thames had fallen to nearly one quarter of its pre-war levels. Shipping was diverted to Liverpool and emergency anchorages in the Clyde, which were more secure from the Luftewaffe. London as a port did provide the services for the assembly of much of the D-Day Landings flotilla in 1944.

By the end of the war many of the essential port facilities had been re-established, although a great deal of rebuilding was left to be carried out. The Upper and Lower Pools suffered particularly badly with quayside warehouses along the north bank of the river, including the Batavia Line berth at Custom House Quay, being destroyed. Much of Hays Wharf on the south Bank was reduced to rubble; nonetheless, reconstruction was addressed as soon as men and materials were available so that the Batavier Line service was reinstated in the Pool in 1947.

Ships of all nations came to the Pool during this post-war period – some more welcome than others. During the Cold War Russian ships were discouraged from coming too far up river for fear that listening devices aboard the ships might tap into the conversation of government. Some ships belonging to GSN that regularly visited East European ports in the Baltic offered a similar service to the British government. The respective masters were not formally told of the arrangement so as not to compromise them as 'spies', but the extra-large 'radar' antenna was something of a give-away. Just what strategic benefit this brought the respective governments is anybody's guess.

The trade of the Pools remained essentially the same in the 1950s and 1960s as it had always been; the Batavia ships still used Custom House Quay, with the United Shipping Company discharging agricultural and dairy products from the Baltic at Fresh Wharf, moving across the river to load. The United Shipping Company was a joint venture created in 1897 by DFDS and Ellerman's Wilson Line initially to serve

St Petersburg, Tallin, Riga and Copenhagen from London. Ellerman's Wilson Line of Hull also provided services from London Millwall Dock and the Upper Pool to Christiansand, Christiana, and other Baltic ports. In the 1890s the *Cameo* and *Albano* were the principal London-based ships, while after the First World War the *Volo* was often at London and in the 1950s any of the standard twelve passenger cargo ships were available for London duties. The Ellerman ships became known as the 'Green Parrots' because they adopted a distinctive dark green hull, making them stand out in the river.

The United Baltic Corporation was still much in evidence above Tower Bridge on the south bank and, of course, the small cargo ships of GSNC were often to be seen from Tower Bridge and elsewhere. Many of the GSN ships were of Dutch design and capable of navigating the many European inland waterways to carry cargoes directly to inland towns and cities. In the Lower Pool and its associated docks, cargo services continued as before to various domestic destinations, with passenger berths available only on the Liverpool service operated by Coast Lines as a holiday opportunity.

United Shipping Company motor cargo ship *Samos* (1947) alongside Sun Wharf in the 1950s.

Ellerman's Wilson Line ran ships to the Baltic from London despite being a partner in the United Shipping Company alongside DFDS. The *Volo* (1890) was a regular visitor to the Pool immediately after the First World War.

GSN's small motor cargo ship *Alouette* (1938) heading down the Thames off Deptford. She was one of a number of Dutch-built vessels specifically designed for service on the Rhine and to other inland ports such as Ghent and Terneuzen. [Andrew Duncan]

Aznar Line's *Monte Ulia* (1952) alongside New Fresh Wharf, directly below London Bridge, in the late 1960s.

New Fresh Wharf hosted fewer refrigerated cargo liners after the Second World War than it had done in the 1930s. However, some deep sea ships still came up to the Pool and this traffic continued until the 1960s. The wharf was, however, used by the Bergen Line cruise ship *Stella Polaris* in July and August 1948 during the Olympic Games that were held in London that summer. This beautiful yacht-like motor ship, which dated from 1927, made a number of trips from Bergen to New Fresh Wharf, allowing visitors to London use of the ship as a hotel during each stop over. While in the Pool the *Stella Polaris* was always dressed overall.

New Fresh Wharf was also host to a new passenger and cargo service to the Canary Islands, which opened in 1952. This service was operated by Naviera Aznar SA of Bilbao with the ships *Monte Ulia* and *Monte Urquoila* – conventional passenger cargo ships with attractive First Class accommodation for the discerning traveller. The *Monte Ulia* was the largest regular visitor to the Upper Pool with a registered gross tonnage of 10,123. Her accommodation was across three decks for 114 passengers in two, four, and six berth cabins, the normal range of public rooms, and a swimming pool. The *Monte Urquoila* had only two decks available to passengers and just fifty-five berths. That goods from the Canaries were being unloaded directly beneath London Bridge must have been a cheery sight to passers-by during those weary years of the early 1950s. The London berth eventually moved down-river to Millwall in the late 1960s.

That the ships came and went, for the most part, without mishap in the crowded tideway is a credit to their officers, pilots and other river users. Many a foreign master in charge of a modest cargo steamer must have breathed a sigh of relief when he passed Gravesend on his way home from the Pool, and again when he finally dropped the pilot and was once again in charge of his ship in open waters.

During the 1950s and 1960s the Pool regained its pre-war buzz and was again a hive of activity. Its trade was very much focussed on the near Continental routes: from the Baltic ports in the north, to the Mediterranean in the south. There was also the important coastal trade and its role as a transhipment service for the long-haul liners tied up in the big docks downstream. Ships in the Pool, from *Lloyd's List*, week beginning Monday 19 August 1957, for example, were recorded as:

Upper Pool:

Alexandra	from Denmark	Symon's Wharf	United Shipping Co.
Ariosto	from Denmark	Chamberlain's Wharf	Ellerman's Wilson Line
Baltrover	from Poland	Mark Brown's Wharf	United Baltic Corporation
Blenda	from Denmark	Cotton's Wharf	United Shipping Co.
Castor	from Holland	Fenning's Wharf	Koninki Nederl. Stoomb. Maats.
Eemstroom	from Holland	Chamber's Wharf	Holland Steamship Co.
Frey	from Sweden	Willson's Wharf	Stockholms Rederi A/B Svea
Heron	from Holland	Irongate Wharf	General Steam Navigation Co.
Hinde	from Holland	Fenning's Wharf	D Nanninga
Holwierde	from Holland	Fenning's Wharf	G Schoorl and others
Jaroslav Dabrowski	from Poland	Mark Brown's Wharf	Polish Ocean Lines
Marocco	from Denmark	William's Wharf	United Shipping Co.
Oranjepolder	from Holland	Custom House Quay	NV Stoomvaart Mij. Westpolder
Rijnstroom	from Holland	Chamber's Wharf	Holland Steamship Co.
Timo	from Holland	Fenning's Wharf	NV Eska

Lower Pool:

British Coast	coastal	Free Trade Wharf	Coast Lines
Broughty	coastal	Dundee Wharf	Dundee, Perth & London Sg. Co.
Clichy	from France	Dundee Wharf	Lockett Wilson Line
Facto	from Norway	Bellamy's Wharf	A/S D/S Facto
Frisian Coast	coastal	Free Trade Wharf	Tyne-Tees Steam Shipping Co.
Gatinais	from France	Colonial Wharf	Cie. Maritime de la Seine
Goldfinch	from Holland	Free Trade Wharf	General Steam Navigation Co.
Gisela Russ	from Germany	Burts Wharf	P/R Gisela Russ
Gwynwood	coastal	Middleton's Wharf	William France, Fenwick & Co.
Hadrian Coast	coastal	Free Trade Wharf	Aberdeen Steam Navigation Co.
Mallard	from France	Victoria Wharf	General Seam Navigation Co.
Lowestoft			
Trader	from Belgium	Anchor Wharf	Great Yarmouth Shipping Co.
Miranda	from Germany	Carron Wharf	A Kirsten & Co.
Nyasa	from Poland	Free Trade Wharf	Polish Steamship Co.
Rifo-an	from Holland	Gibb's Wharf	D Buining
St Antonius	from Germany	Carron Wharf	Johann Schepers
Sir Leonard			
Pearce	coastal	Brunswick Wharf	Central Electricity Authority
Stork	from Holland	Free Trade Wharf	General Steam Navigation Co.
Titania	from Germany	Aberdeen Wharf	A Kirsten & Co.
Texel	from Holland	Morocco Wharf	NV Scheepvaart Mij. 'Triton'
Velazquez	from Spain	Butler's Wharf	MacAndrews & Co.

London Dock:

Arcturus	from Norway	Det Bergenske Dampskibsselskab
Beachy	coastal	Clyde Shipping Co.
Darinian	from Mediterranean ports	Ellerman Lines
Edinburgh Merchant	coastal	London Scottish Lines
Grindefjell	from Norway	A/S Luksefjell
Ireland	from Portugal	Curry Line
Meise	from Germany	Argo Line
Mira	from Finland	Finska Angfartygs Ab (Finland Line)
Pacheco	from Spain	MacAndrews & Co.
Polomares	from Mediterranean	MacAndrews & Co.
Sandpiper	from Portugal	General Steam Navigation Company
Schwalbe	from Germany	Argo Line
Toward	coastal	Clyde Shipping Co.
Westerdok	from Holland	NV Zeevaart Maarts'

Shadwell Basin:

City of Brussels	from Belgium	City of Brussels Steamship Co.
Ponzano	from Mediterranean	MacAndrews & Co.
Villegas	from Mediterranean	MacAndrews & Co.

Regent's Canal basin:

Polly M	coastal	Metcalfe Motor Coasters
Walcrag	from Holland	Walford Lines
Woodcock	from Germany	General Steam Navigation Co.
Woodwren	from Holland	General Steam Navigation Co.

Wapping Basin:

Paulina	from Germany	A Kirsten & Co.

Ships waited at the buoys off Tower Stairs, as indeed the *Frey* had done over the weekend, until their berth in the Upper Pool became available. Buoys were also available down-river for incoming ships awaiting vacation of their berths by departing vessels. By the Friday of the week beginning 23 August a further seven ships had arrived in the Upper Pool, replacing vessels that had sailed. Newcomers included the *Batavier II* now berthed at Customs House Quay and *Batavier III* at Chamberlain's Wharf, both on Wm H. Muller's direct service to Rotterdam, and United Shipping Company's *Primula* inbound from Helsingborg and *Diana* from Copenhagen, both with chilled dairy products, and the Dutchman *Amstelstroom* from Amsterdam. The Lower Pool had also received an influx of fourteen new ships by Friday. GSN's *Hirondelle* was working cargo from Groningen at Butler's Wharf, along with the *Valdes* belonging to MacAndrews & Co. and inbound from Mediterranean ports, having also called at Lisbon.

Coast Lines had long since moved from its base in Shadwell Basin in favour of Free Trade Wharf. It also had a berth in the East India Dock which the ships of subsidiary company the Channel Isles Shipping Company shared. However, transhipment cargoes, to and from the deep sea liners in the main docks, brought in from Liverpool and Scotland formed an important part of normal inventories and the Coast Lines flag was often seen in the main dock systems with the coasters lying alongside cargo liners, loading and unloading goods. Transhipment cargoes had been badly hit in the depression between the wars as Hancock described:

> In London the charges remained so high that there was a tendency for merchandise which, in the past, had been transhipped there, to be diverted to Continental ports, and for cargo which formerly came from the continent in steamers direct to London to find its way through the outports.

Rotterdam was one such 'output' that gained from London – a port that benefited from its huge hinterland, which traversed the entire catchment of the River Rhine and beyond. Trade between London and Rotterdam consequently developed out of all proportion to trade with other near Continental ports.

However, all this was about to change as the 1960s drew to a close. Containerisation and the roll-on roll-off vehicle ferry were soon to kill all trade into and out of the Pool of London – a death knell that was a sudden as it was unforeseen.

Chapter 4

The Sailing Ships and Packets

The larger and heavier vessels of the Honourable East India Company could not come up beyond Blackwall; even when the East India Dock was opened, the big wooden-walls had to anchor in the river and part discharge their cargoes before they could lock in. Goods came up to London in heavily guarded caravans, some also by sailing hoy to Poolside quays. From the early nineteenth century privately-owned sailing ships were chartered into the East India franchise but these were built to a much lighter design than the East Indiamen and tended to leak badly during the stresses of loading and unloading. Their Chinese crew had to be retained on board to man the pumps overnight, crews and all hands otherwise being out of bounds in the docks during night time hours.

The West India trade was better suited to the available wharfage in the Pool, with smaller ships of shallower draught than their East India counterparts. However, few of them came right up to the Pool – many unloading in the river below Deptford as they tended to arrive in convoys and available wharf and dock space was limited.

An indication of the variety of trade at the start of the nineteenth century is given by the toll fees levied on entry to the new London Dock (fees for cargo handling and landing taxes were additional):

First Class: Vessels trading coastwise, including colliers, 1s per ton.
Second Class: vessels trading to Ireland, the North Sea, and the English Channel, 1s 3d per ton.
Third Class: vessels trading to the Baltic and Archangel, 1s 6d per ton.
Fourth Class: Vessels trading to South of Ushant, the west coast of Spain and Portugal, and Newfoundland, 1s 9d per ton.
Fifth Class: Vessels trading to the Mediterranean, Africa, and America, 2s per ton.
Sixth Class: Vessels trading to the East Indies, Persia, and China, 2s 6d per ton.

A twenty-one-year concession was given to the dock owners so that all tobacco, rice, wine and brandy – except that from the East and West Indies – had to be landed at London Dock.

The three-masted sailing ship *Free Trader* discharging cargo in London Dock. [From an etching by E. W. Cooke, 1829]

The arrival of the London Packet at Leith, Edinburgh, 1822.

The domestic sailing packets maintained the important link between London and the provincial coastal centres in the eighteenth and early nineteenth centuries. The need for this link was greatly enhanced by the onset of the Industrial Revolution and for good communication between centres and exchange of materials and manufactured goods.

One of the earliest established routes was between Symon's Wharf and the upper Humber to the ports of Armine and Goole and in 1765 this service switched to Stanton's Wharf under the aegis of William France. The sailing brigs maintained a regular service to and from London – a service that was taken over by steam in the mid-nineteenth century for what had then become France, Fenwick & Company, and that only left Stanton's Wharf in favour of Free Trade Wharf in 1926.

In the late eighteenth century, the traditional route for passengers and goods travelling between London and Scotland was sailing smack to Berwick, and then north overland to either Edinburgh or Glasgow. The east coast passage is far shorter than the west coast and direct services between London and Glasgow through the Irish Sea became viable only in the steam era. Sailing smacks served between Liverpool and Bristol and between Bristol and South Coast ports but there was no direct link with London, other than from selected ports on the South Coast. There was, however, a weekly service by smack from Belfast to London managed by Langtrys and Hardman although this was not introduced until the late 1820s. Meanwhile the East Coast ports such as Yarmouth, Lynn, Hull, and the Tyne and Wear, were comparatively well served with direct connections to the capital (Chapter 6).

The east coast sailing smacks and schooners running between the Pool and various Scottish ports are good examples of the vessels operating early coastal services. Fast sailing smacks were used for the regular service between Berwick and London from 1753 when the Union Company was incorporated. In 1802 the company extended its service to Leith, and in 1809 Edinburgh merchants formed the London & Edinburgh Shipping Company 'for the purpose of establishing a regular and superior means of communication between Leith and London'. The new company absorbed the goodwill and assets of the old Union Company and quickly provided ten new and fast smacks that were built at Leith in 1810, with five more smacks added during the period 1816 to 1827. Casualties were high and at least two of the fleet were lost during the 1820s, there being virtually no aids to navigation then in place along the East Coast.

Samuel Garbett & Company maintained a fleet of sloops running between Bo'ness near Edinburgh and east coast ports as far as London from 1763 to 1772. However, mounting debts allowed the Carron Shipping Company of Falkirk to buy the sloops. The majority shareholder of Samuel Garbett & Company, the Honourable William Elphinstone, later chairman of the East India Company, sold out to the Carron Company of Falkirk in 1782. The Carron Company owned a large ironworks near Falkirk, initially producing ploughshares and cannonballs, and later the carronade, the highly successful short cannon. Under Carron Company ownership the sloops each carried a cannonball at the top of the mainmast, supposedly the signal 'I am carrying carronades', but later very much as the company trademark. The sloops, and in due course also schooners, carried cast-iron goods south to London, eventually unleashing the cast-iron bathtub on the Victorian Londoners. The ships carried transhipments from the East India Company as well as goods from southern England northwards. In the early nineteenth century an indication of the politics of Europe was that concessionary fares were offered to 'men of arms' who were willing to defend vessels that might be attacked by French privateers.

An intense four-times-weekly service was built up between Bo'ness and London. It partly transferred to Grangemouth in 1850 once its ships had outgrown the smaller port, but moving away from sail only in 1852 when it commissioned its first sea-going steamship.

Local merchants formed the Dundee Shipping Company at Dundee in 1798 to provide sailing smacks to serve between Perth and Dundee, and south to the Pool of London. Rivals in the same trade – John Richardson & Company of Perth – were bought out in 1806 to form the Dundee & Perth Shipping Company. However, in 1807 a new company was established and bitter rivalry developed between the smacks of the established operator on the route and the newcomer, the Tay Shipping Company. Competition was short-lived, and two of the three smart new smacks of Tay Shipping Co. were bought and placed in service with Dundee & Perth Shipping Co. Peace reigned until 1819, when yet another rival was formed in the shape of the Dundee & Perth Union Shipping Company. The year 1826 saw the merger of the rivals, with the younger company precipitating the merger by advertising its vessels as 'best suited for the London trade'.

There was also the problem of which company wharf on the Thames should be retained and which disposed of. The expensive compromise was reached that Hore's Wharf would become the inbound wharf and the adjacent Downe's Wharf (both on the site of what later became the London & Continental Steam Wharf in the Lower Pool) for departures. The new company was in a strong position, developing also services via the Forth & Clyde Canal to Glasgow. Its average six-day trip to London was well patronised and the company saw no immediate need to turn to steam. Even though it started to offer a steam packet service in 1830, under duress from a competitor, it continued to buy new schooners until 1857.

Although sail remained the dominant form of transport, the steamship arrived on the Leith to London route as early as 1821. Though the wooden paddle steamer *City of Edinburgh* was fêted on her first arrival at Leith, her erratic schedule, interspersed with prolonged and unannounced maintenance periods, did little to endear her to the travelling public; besides, poor weather required her to stay in port while the sailing smacks and schooners continued regardless.

As trade developed on the Edinburgh route, so merchants and passengers transferred their allegiance to the steamships. The fruits of the recent industrial revolution provided cargoes aplenty, with many goods destined for onward transhipment at the port of destination. But there was still room for sail and the London & Edinburgh Shipping Company (rather than its former competitor the Steam Packet Company) commissioned a series of clippers built in Aberdeen in the 1840s. The 'Aberdeen Clippers' were given classic names that included the *Nonsuch, Rapid, Dart,* and *Swift,* and it was these ships that replaced the old schooners – the last of which was disposed of in 1849. The Aberdeen Steam Navigation Company took delivery of its last sailing schooner only in 1846.

It is noteworthy that all the sailing packets were owned outside London. This suggests that the need for the provinces to communicate with London was far greater than that for London to talk to its provinces. This was to change when the steamship arrived as the newly created and London-based General Steam Navigation Company then made significant inroads into the various East Coast monopolies. The eventual dominance of the General Steam Navigation Company in the Upper and Lower Pools was described by Cope Cornford's *A Century of Sea Trading 1824 to 1924*:

The General Steam Navigation Company rent a part of St Katherine Dock; and their cargoes are neatly stored in the open lower storey, white-washed and clean like a monastery, and above it in the chambers of the warehouse. The company's Belgian,

Below Bridge, *c.* 1830, from a contemporary engraving.

Dutch, Northern France and east coast cargoes are loaded and discharged at the quays inside St Katherine Dock and adjacent to it, at the British & Foreign Wharf, Harrison's Wharf and Carron Wharf, so that their berths extend for over half a mile, from Tower bridge down-stream to St George's Stairs.

The company also use loading and discharging berths at the north, south and east quays in the London Dock, on the south side of the river, at Butler's Wharf; and on the north side of the river above Tower Bridge, at Fresh Wharf, which lies immediately below London Bridge [and at Brewers Wharf adjacent to the Tower]. The company also owns another quay, Irongate which lies immediately below the Tower.

The collier trade was important. The masters of the small sailing brigs, the 'Geordie colliers', loaded coal at the coal ports in north-east England and brought it down to the Pool to be lifted out into barges from which it was sold to the agents in London. At any one time there could be several-hundred small colliers unloading in the Pool, especially if they had been holed up at Yarmouth Roads or at Harwich waiting for the south-west wind to abate.

An attempt had been made in the 1820s to get the colliers into a special dock and off the river to ease navigation in its crowded waters. However, the collier owners were not enamoured by the dues likely at this new facility and remained in the river where the ships were used as a floating warehouse selling their wares. Once the East & West India Dock Railway had been completed to Blackwall in the early 1850s, however, the colliers did move to their own collier dock and unloaded directly into barges or rail trucks. The retreat of the sailing colliers from the Pool allowed free movement of lighters up from the docks and better navigation for ships in the river. It also coincided with the introduction of better-equipped wharves and mechanised cargo-handling gear, although ships still also worked cargo in mid-river to lighters.

By the early 1850s the east coast coal trade was in a bad way – it was suffering from competition from rail transport that was opening up the coalfield in the English Midlands and maintaining a steady and increasing stock of fuel available to the

Metropolis. The now-outdated Geordie collier was little match for such competition and in a short space of time steam colliers began to dominate the trade, the pioneer steamer being the *John Bowes* (Chapter 5).

The variety of trade in the London Dock is encapsulated in this letter to the *Morning Chronicle*, 1849, by Henry Mayhew:

> As you enter the dock, the sight of the forest of masts in the distance, and the tall chimneys vomiting clouds of black smoke, and the many-coloured flags flying in the air, has a most peculiar effect; while the sheds, with the monster wheels arching through the roofs, look like the paddle-boxes of huge steamers. Along the quay you see now men with their faces blue with indigo, and now gaugers with their long brass-tipped rule dripping with spirit from the cask they have been probing; then will come a group of flaxen-haired sailors, chattering German; and next a black sailor, with a cotton handkerchief twisted turban-like around his head. Presently a blue-smocked butcher, with fresh meat and a bunch of cabbages in the tray on his shoulder, and shortly afterwards a mate with green parakeets in a wooden cage. Here you will see sitting on a bench a sorrowful-looking woman, with new bright cooking tins at her feet, telling you she is an emigrant preparing for her voyage. As you pass along this quay the air is pungent with tobacco, at that it overpowers you with fumes of rum. Then you are nearly sickened with the stench of hides and huge bins of horns, and shortly afterwards the atmosphere is fragrant with coffee and spice.
>
> Nearly everywhere you meet stacks of cork, or else yellow bins of sulphur or lead-coloured copper ore. As you enter this warehouse, the flooring is sticky, as if it had been newly tarred, with the sugar that has leaked through the casks, and as you descend into the dark vaults you see long lines of lights hanging from the black arches, and lamps flitting about midway. Here you sniff the fumes of the wine, and there the peculiar fungus smell of dry-rot. Then the jumble of sounds as you pass along the dock blends in anything but sweet concord. The sailors are singing boisterous songs from the Yankee ship just entering, the cooper is hammering at the casks on the quay, the chains of the cranes, loosed of their weight, rattle as they fly up again; the ropes splash in the water; some captain shouts his orders through his hands; a goat bleats from some ship in the basin; and empty casks roll along the stones with a hollow drum-like sound. Here the heavy laden ships are down far below the quay, and you descend to them by ladders, whilst in another basin they are high up out of the water, so that their green copper sheathing is almost level with the eye of the passenger, while above his head a long line of bowsprits stretch far over the quay, and from them hang spars and planks as a gangway to each ship.

The deep sea ships that came up to the Pool itself included some of the very famous clipper ships. Following the Tooley Street Fire in June 1861, the owner of Hay's Wharf, John Humphrey, had to seek financial help to reconstruct his buildings. He went to Hugh Colin Smith and Arthur Magniac, who were the agents for Jardine

The *Flying Spur* (1860) arriving at Hay's Dock in October 1862 with tea from Foochow. [From an oil painting by Gordon Ellis]

The tea clipper *Taeping* (1863). [From an oil painting by Jack Spurling]

Matheson's China Trade, and who then became partners of John Humphrey. As a result, Hay's Wharf became the unloading and loading point for Jardine's famous clippers and the first of these to berth at Hay's Dock was the *Flying Spur* in October 1862, with a full cargo of China tea. Most of the other clippers, however, used the West India Dock.

The last of the Great Tea Races took place in 1866 when the clipper ship *Taeping* arrived in London Dock on the same tide as the *Ariel* and *Serica*, although they docked in the East India and West India Docks respectively. The three sailing clippers left Foo Chow together ninety-nine days previously.

The deep sea sailing ship remained very much in evidence. Even in the 1890s the Shadwell Basin and London Dock were host to sailing ships belonging to the Loch Line, Devitt & Moore, Trinder Anderson, Shaw Savill & Company, George Thompson,

Alex Nichol, Donaldson Rose, Carmichael, John Willis, George Duncan & Company and many others. Captain T. Findlay wrote in *Sea Breezes*, October 1949:

The *Torrens*, under Captain Angel was a frequent visitor to the London Dock. I remember seeing her haul out of Shadwell Basin bound for Adelaide, her decks lumbered up with livestock: geese, chickens, pigs, and a cow to supply fresh milk for the passengers she carried. She was a composite built ship with teak planking and had a poop 80 feet long. Built in 1875 by James Laing at Sunderland, her registered tonnage was 1,276. I remember seeing the *Samuel Plimsoll* inward from Sydney with the wool clip for the January sales – a fine looking ship. Her crew were walking round the capstan heaving her into the locks singing the famous shanty 'We're homeward bound'...

Strolling further along the dock... we came to a fine four-masted barque, the *Amazon*, sugar-laden from Manila. Next was one of Dunlop's Clans, the four-masted *Clan Graham*, of Glasgow. Then the *Dharwar*, owned by John Willis, who also owned the *Cutty Sark*; a fine strongly-built ship, the former arrived from Melbourne. Next to her and from Sydney was the *Mount Stewart*, a lofty skysail-yarder, Captain Green in command...

Ice and sailing ships on the river off Customs House Quay 1879. [*The Graphic*]

The *Torrens* (1875) was an immigrant ship on the Australian run with First Class passengers accommodated under the 80-foot-long poop and Second Class in the 'tween decks foreword.

The famous wool clipper
Mount Stewart (1891). [From a
contemporary oil painting]

The Regent's Canal Dock at this time was home to the 'ice and timber droghers' inbound from Norway and elsewhere. The ice was a seasonal import and bought from the ship by ice cream and fish vendors throughout London, whereas the timber imports from Scandinavia continued regardless of season and weather in whatever old sailing ship was available to carry the load.

But, as time went on, the sailing ships slowly dropped out of the long-haul trades and the steamship became the universal workhorse. In the end a sailing ship arrival in the river was greeted with nostalgia by those that remembered 'the good old days', until only the odd Thames sailing barge frequented the Pool and its associated docks.

The last commercial arrival of a large sailing ship in London was that of the four-masted barque *Pamir*, in December 1947, inbound from Auckland. She discharged in the Victoria Dock before moving to the Shadwell Basin for repairs and later returning from Antwerp to New Zealand. She was originally one of the famous German-owned 'Flying Ps' and was built in 1905; much use was made of powered winches for handling sails and she was equipped with steel ropes throughout. The ship foundered at sea with heavy loss of life in 1957, having earlier sailed from Buenos Aires with a cargo of grain.

Many years later, in July 1989, a major celebration of sail took place before the start of the Tall Ships Race across the North Sea. This was the very last time that such a large pageant of sail could be witnessed from Tower Bridge – an eloquent reminder of the commercial past of that part of the river. Some 140 sail training ships from fifteen countries assembled in the Upper and Lower Pools, including a number of square rigged vessels, as Robert Simper explained in *Sea Breezes*, September 1989:

> In the Lower Pool, the Polish full-rigged ship *Dar Mlodziezy*, with a crew of 230, and the Russian *Kruzenshtern*, with a crew of 236, towered above the German barque *Alexander von Humbolt*, with 60 crew. This new German barque, a former Kiel light vessel, has a green hull and incredible green sails and it was the first time she had been in a Tall Ships Race from a British port. Other newcomers were the Portuguese four-masted schooner *Creoula*, the Polish brigantine *Henry Rutkowski*, the Oman

The Russian four-masted barque *Kruzenshtern* (1926) in the Lower Pool in 1989 before the start of the Tall Ships Race. She is still in use as a training ship.

barquentine *Shabab Oman*, originally the British schooner *Captain Scott* and now with white-painted hull and spars, and the Swedish ketch *Norem*, just to name but a few.

The mail was always regularly and nearly always reliably delivered to the ships lying in the Pool, as described by F. Z. Claro in an article that first appeared in *Sea Breezes*, April 1966.

In 1793 in the reign of George III, one of the watermen applied to the Postmaster general asking for a special appointment as ships' postman to deliver letters to vessels in the Thames in the Pool of London... The application was refused by the authorities. A few years later in 1799, William Simpson, a fireman of the Hand in Hand Insurance Company, was appointed as the official ships' postman, delivering and collecting correspondence from ships in the tideway.

He was instructed to blow a posthorn when approaching ships for delivery and to warn them to have letters ready for collection. All went well for a few years until 1806 when he had an accident on duty by falling down an uncovered hold. His son, also William Simpson, took his place until he stole various letters and went into hiding. The Post Office offered £100 reward for news of his whereabouts in August 1810. This felony at the time was a capital offence with the death sentence. Simpson was caught by the Bow Street Runners after a hue and cry at East Grinstead, Sussex The jury [at the subsequent trial] recommended mercy as he was a young man 20 years of age, and the sentence was amended by the Crown to 'transportation for life overseas'

During the search for Simpson, Samuel Evans had been acting as assistant ships' postman and for over 150 years son followed father, until Herbert Evans, the last of the family retired in 1952. In all, over the years, there were six members of the family who performed this service to vessels in the Pool of London, in war or peace, whatever the weather or state of the tide – a record unique in the story of ships' postmen anywhere in the long history of the Post Office.

Chapter 5

Pioneer Steamships

Until the arrival of the steam packet, communication between the Pool at London and the major centres along the south Thames coast was by sailing packet. These were known as the 'Margate Hoy', and the 'Long Ferry' to Gravesend, and a 'tilt' boat – a rowing boat with an awning or tilt – was used for the journey. Dependent on favourable winds and tides, the hoy could take up to a week to get down river to Margate, with calls at Gravesend and Sheerness. A little wooden paddle steamer, however, could guarantee arrival at Margate the same day and a return trip to Hammersmith by evening the next day. But the last of the tilt boats, the *Duke of York*, was only withdrawn in 1834 when the smoky steamship finally reigned supreme. Travel to centres in Essex, however, remained dependent on the stage coach, with access to the river hindered by Dickens' famous Essex Marshes, although small boats could get to both Chelmsford and Colchester.

One of the first steamers to be seen at London was the *Richmond*, owned by George Dodd. She was a small river paddler and was placed on a service between Richmond and Hammersmith in 1814, just two years after the successful trials of Henry Bell's *Comet* on the Clyde, and one year before the end of the Napoleonic Wars. The little *Richmond* had a 10 horsepower engine; the 'great frost' of 1814/1815 did little to help her battles against the tides when the river froze over at Blackfriars. When a steam pipe burst, the Watermen made loud claims that the steam engine was a danger to all and that the *Richmond* should not be allowed on the river. The coming of the steamer had not been welcomed by the Watermen and boatmen of the Thames, who immediately recognised that their very existence could be under threat, and who did everything they could to hinder the progress and acceptance of the new technology, as Norman Fox described in *The Illustrated London News*, January 1971:

…the watermen obstructed the paddle steamers at every turn, with bills introduced in Parliament and more literal and effective obstructions placed in the river. The fact was that the public had been won over, and the steamers thrived. Owners attempted to run 'through' services from Richmond to Margate and competition became intense and dangerous. Racing was the cause of more than one fatal accident, yet the popularity of the steamers increased.

The first sea-going packet was the wooden paddle steamer *Marjory*, which arrived from her builders on the Clyde in January 1815, having travelled via the Forth & Clyde Canal and then down the North Sea coast. Her arrival in the Pool marked the entry of the steamship into service on the lower Thames services. It also heralded a long association between Clyde shipbuilders and the owners of the steam packets and subsequent excursion ships that have since served the Thames piers 'weather and other circumstances permitting'. The *Marjory* was placed on service from Wapping Old Stairs in the Pool to Milton, where passengers landed by rowing boat. The return trip lasted over two days and cost a substantial 8s in the chief cabin but only 4s in the fore cabin.

An advertisement for the *Marjory* on her first sailing on 23 January 1815 read:

> The public are respectfully informed that the new London steam engine packet *Marjory*, Captain Cortis, will start precisely at ten o'clock, on Monday morning, the twenty third inst. from Wapping Old Stairs, near the London Dock, to Milton, below Gravesend, and will return from thence at the same hour on the succeeding morning to the same stairs, the said packet having superb accommodation. Passengers and their luggage will be conveyed to and fro with more certain speed and safety, than by any other conveyance by land or water, and on reasonable fares. Passengers are requested to be punctual to the time specified.

The *Marjory* tended to miss a lot of sailings, laid up either at Milton or at Wapping while her machinery was repaired and adjusted. To add to the difficulties, Captain Cortis was removed from his vessel and replaced by a Freeman of the Waterman's Company following proceedings under the Waterman's Act. Not surprisingly, this pioneer vessel was withdrawn at the end of the summer.

The next steamer to be introduced was the *Argyle*, sometimes reported as the *Duke of Argyle*. The *Argyle* joined the so-called 'Long Ferry' to Gravesend, providing a daily service each way for her new owners, R. Cheesewright & Company. As with the *Marjory*, she had a carvel hull, and a large square sail could be set on the tall funnel pipe under favourable weather conditions. Her engine consisted of a single vertical cylinder of 24 inches diameter and the piston had a stroke of 36 inches. The cabins opened on to an outside gallery which, with her gun ports, made the *Argyle* an imposing sight (the French were still considered a threat at that time, the Admiralty preferring to arm merchantmen in readiness for renewed war). She was, by all accounts, both well-appointed and well received. *The Times* reported on her arrival into service in July 1815:

> She [the *Argyle*] is rapid, spacious, and indeed a splendid vessel. Her cabins are large and fitted with all that elegance could suggest or that personal comfort could require. She presents a choice library, and back gammon, draught boards, and other amusements are provided. For the express purpose of combining delicacy with comfort, a stewardess tends on the fair sex.

It was not long before other steamers took up service. There were four at the close of 1815 – the *Richmond, Argyle, Defiance* and *Hope*. The *Defiance* was employed between the Pool and Margate and the *Hope* ran to Sheerness and Chatham. The *Argyle*, renamed the *Thames*, served Gravesend and Margate for the Gravesend Steam Packet. The following year she was replaced by a faster and larger vessel, the *Regent*, 112 tons and engines of 24 nominal horsepower, notable as the first steam boat to have been built on the Thames at a total cost of £11,000. Her designer was none other than Isambard Brunel. However, just over a year after entering the Margate service, she was gutted by fire off Whitstable when the funnel became too hot and started to fall apart causing the deck to set alight. Fortunately her captain was able to beach her and put his forty passengers and crew of ten ashore.

The Gravesend service operated by the *Thames* was advertised as follows:

> The *Thames*, Captain Payne, will leave the Tower Stairs for Gravesend every morning at 8 o'clock (Friday excepted) and return every afternoon at 3 o'clock the same day for London. Fares on Sundays 3/- each, other days best cabin 3/-, fore cabin 2/-. Refreshments provided: tea, bottled porter, etc.

The *Thames* offered a long outside gallery onto which the cabins opened. This gave her a majestic appearance, which, coupled with the formidable aspect of her row of gun ports, made an impressive picture.

As the steamship became accepted as a more or less reliable form of transport, a number of small companies were set up to operate them. It was not uncommon for the majority shareowner to double as ship's master, ownership being divided on the 1/64th principle. Some companies such as the Gravesend Steam Packet owned and operated more than one ship. In the first ten years of steamship operation, twenty-six steamers had seen service on the Thames so that in 1824, at least fifteen steamers were on service to Gravesend, Sheerness and Chatham, Southend-on-Sea landing stage (until 1830 just a wooden jetty accessible only at high water), Ramsgate and the fishing port of Margate; all of these operated from the Pool.

Some of the early packets were distinctive, some failed from the outset, while others gave up to forty years of service on the river. Among the failures was the *London Engineer*. Burtt (1949) describes the ship as follows:

> Her dimensions were 120 feet long, beam 24 feet, with a draft of 5 feet, tonnage 315. The machinery was of peculiar design, being of the bell crank pattern, having two vertical cylinders 36 inches in diameter with a 30 inch stroke. The cylinders were placed on either side of the vessel driving a pair of internal paddle wheels. The two paddles made 28 revolutions per minute, and the stream of water to them was kept constant by air forced into the waterway by two large pumps. The boiler pressure was 5 lb per square inch and steam was supplied by three single-furnace copper boilers.

The *London Engineer* was nicely appointed with upholstered settees in the main cabin, although fore cabin occupants had to make do with wooden benches. She was flush-decked, as were all her contemporaries, but she had a highly ornamented hull, looking to all intents and purpose like a screw steamer. There was ornate scroll work fore and aft, a bowsprit and a figurehead – the latter best described as a woman wringing her hands (perhaps she knew all along that the ship could not be steered in a straight line or got fully up to speed!). The ship's funnel was nearly as tall as her two masts. However, she did not go anywhere fast, and her working career on the Margate run was brief.

Rogue designs continued to be commissioned long into the steam era. A notorious example was the twin-hulled steamer *Gemini*, built in 1850 to cream off some of the anticipated traffic during the London Exhibition of 1851. Alas, despite plush accommodation for 1,000 passengers, she could make no headway against the tide and could gain no steerage. Her trial trip was her last, leaving her inventor and owner £14,000 worse off. Why nobody had trialled such a radical design at a small scale is anybody's guess.

One of the fastest of the early packets was the *Favourite*, her name seemingly an early attempt at marketing. In 1818 the *Favourite* accomplished the first 'day trip' to Margate from London; sailing at 4.45 a.m. she reached Margate at 2 p.m. and started the return trip 45 minutes later. She returned her 158 passengers safely to the city at 10 p.m.

A newspaper article entitled 'Early Steamboat Travelling: A Voyage to Margate in 1823' and published in 1895 included this description of travelling aboard the *Venus* operated by the Margate Company and later by GSN:

> ... on board the *Venus* steamboat for Margate when boiling and smoking away in the most agreeable style to the great delight of nearly two hundred cockneys of all ages, sizes and sexes. She (if feminine is the gender of a steamer) arrived in 7½ hours at her destination. The accommodation of this vessel is superior to any sailing vessel I ever saw. Splendid cabins, mahogany fittings, horsehair sofas, carpeted floors, tiers of windows like the ports of a frigate, with bars and bar maids, kitchen and cooks, stewards and waiters and all suitable paraphernalia of splendid breakfasting and dinnering...

The *Royal Sovereign* and *Hero* were very much the market leaders when delivered from the yard of Thomas Brockelbank at Deptford in the early 1820s. These vessels were over 130 feet long with gross tonnages of 220 and 233 respectively. However, their most distinguishing feature was that they were the first Thames steamers to have engines that could develop as much as 100 nominal horsepower. Such larger and faster vessels were the direct response to demand, with over a million passengers now using the Thames packets every year. As was the custom of the day, they still carried twelve-pounder guns concealed behind ornamented ports.

In the immediate years after its formation in 1824, GSN added five new dedicated Thames steamers to its fleet: the *Eclipse* and *Attwood* in 1825, *Columbine* and *Harlequin* in 1826, and the *Ramona* in 1829. Of these the *Harlequin* and *Columbine* are notable as having the most powerful engines, generating 140 nominal horsepower, whereas the engines aboard the *Eclipse* generated only 70. Other vessels, such as the

Ostende   *Entrée du Port (d'après une ancienne estampe) dated 1833*

Nels, Bruxelles Serie 28 No. 131

GSN's *Earl of Liverpool* (1824) from a contemporary sketch of her entering Ostend harbour. [DP World]

Earl of Liverpool, were used to develop the near European trade. No further vessels were built specifically for Thames service until 1844, although second-hand ships were bought, while the company enjoyed a period of consolidation. The prestige service remained the daily return to Margate, as advertised for the *Eclipse* in the early days of the company:

> Every weekday from the Hungerford Market Pier at 7.30 a.m., calling at Old Swan Pier at 7.45 a.m., Tunnel Pier 8.00 a.m. and Greenwich 8.30 a.m. for Herne Bay and Margate. Directly the steamer starts an excellent plain breakfast can be obtained in the chief cabin, 1/- each, ham eggs etc. are plentifully supplied at a trifling additional charge. An excellent band of music is on board.

The *Eclipse* was scheduled to arrive at Herne Bay at 12.45 p.m. and Margate at 1.30 p.m. throughout the summer season. With a fifteen minute turnaround at Margate, the return arrival at Hungerford Market Pier was at 8.00 p.m. – a service requiring an average speed of over twelve knots. The *Harlequin* and *Columbine* were the mainstay of a new service from Custom House to Margate and Ramsgate, at *6s* return. They were later lengthened and were used in the 1840s for the Calais and Boulogne services and occasionally also to Le Havre. The Boulogne service cost just £1 and allowed passengers 48 hours ashore.

Before overland transport became comfortable and safe, the preferred way to travel around Britain was by sea. The first coastal sea-going steam packet to serve

The Public are respectfully informed, that the undermentioned

FIRST CLASS AND POWERFUL

STEAM PACKETS

Start for the following Ports, & usually perform the passages in the times stated, every month,

From off the Custom-house or Tower,

LONDON.

LISBON & GIBRALTAR, *The George the Fourth,* 760 tons, and 150 horse.power, P. BLACK, Commander, and *The Duke of York,* 760 tons, and 150 horse power, J. MOWLE, Commander, touching at Vigo and Oporto, and for the convenience of those Passengers who cannot embark at Deptford, the vessel will call off Brighton, and at Portsmouth, on three days notice being given at the Office. Fares, including provisions and attendance, from London to Gibraltar, Chief Cabin £31. 10s. Fore Cabin £26.—From London to Lisbon, Oporto, or Vigo, Chief Cabin £25. Fore Cabin £20. Carriages, horses, and merchandize, by agreement.

BOULOGNE, in fifteen hours, *The Rapid,* CAPTAIN JENNINGS, every Tuesday and Friday, returning every Sunday and Wednesday.—Chief Cabin 37s. Fore Cabin 26s. Carriages, four wheels £4. 10s. two wheels £3. horses £4. and dogs 5s. each.

CALAIS, in twelve hours, *The Attwood,* CAPTAIN STRANACK, and *The Lord Melville,* CAPTAIN MIDDLETON, every Monday, Wednesday, Thursday, and Saturday.—Chief Cabin 33s. Fore Cabin 22s. 6d. Four-wheel carriages £4. 4s. two-wheel ditto £2. 2s. horses £3. 3s. and dogs 5s. each.

OSTEND, in sixteen hours, *The Earl of Liverpool,* CAPTAIN PEAKE, and *Mountaineer,* CAPTAIN MATE, every Wednesday and Saturday.—Chief Cabin 40s. Fore Cabin 30s. Four wheel carriages £4. 4s. two wheel ditto £2. 2s. horses £4. 4s. and dogs 5s. each.

ROTTERDAM; in twenty-six hours, *The Belfast,* CAPTAIN ROBERTS, every Saturday morning at nine o'clock, returning every Tuesday at ten.—Chief Cabin £2. 10s. Fore Cabin £1. 15s. Horses £6s. 6s. dogs 10s. carriages £6. 6s. chariots £5. 5s. gigs £3. 3s. Freight on merchandize by agreement. N. B. On the arrival of the packet at Rotterdam, a Diligence is in readiness to convey the passengers to the Hague.

HAMBURG, in fifty-four hours, *The Sir Edward Banks,* CAPTAIN HOWLETT, and *The Hylton Jolliffe,* CAPTAIN MOWLL, every Saturday morning at seven precisely, and starts from Hamburg, every Saturday early in the morning.—Chief Cabin £9. Fore Cabin £7. Four wheel carriages £10. two wheel ditto £6. 6s. Horses £8. 8s. dogs £1. each. Freight on merchandise by agreement.

FROM BRIGHTON PIER.

TO DIEPPE, in eight hours, *The Eclipse,* CAPTAIN CHEESEMAN, *The Talbot,* CAPTAIN NORWOOD, and the Brighton Company's Packet, *Quentin Durward,* every Monday, Tuesday, Wednesday, Thursday and Friday.—Chief Cabin 40s. Fore Cabin 30s. Carriages £1. 1s. per wheel. Horses £3. 3s. and dogs 5s. each.——Should the weather render it inconvenient for the Passengers to embark at Brighton Pier, the Packet will start from Newhaven, & timely notice thereof will be given by the Agent at Brighton.

FROM LONDON TO MARGATE AND RAMSGATE, *The Harlequin,* CAPTAIN CORBIN, *City of London,* CAPTAIN MARTIN, *Columbine,* CAPTAIN GRANT, and *The Royal Sovereign,* CAPT. MAJOR. For MARGATE, every morning at nine o'clock, (Sunday excepted), and to RAMSGATE every Wednesday and Saturday mornings at eight o'clock.

Season Tickets £3. 3s. with the privilege of the *Ramsgate* or *Margate* Packets, may be had of the Captains on board.—Chief Cabin 12s. Fore Cabin 10s. Children under twelve years, and servants attending families, 6s. each.

REFRESHMENTS MAY BE HAD ON BOARD.

ALL THE PACKETS HAVE ELEGANT STATE CABINS FOR THE LADIES, AND FEMALE ATTENDANTS.

Carriages, horses, and baggage belonging to passengers, to and from foreign Ports, shipped and landed free of expence at Custom-house Quay, London.

No merchandize can be taken by the Packets to and from foreign Ports without special agreement.

Information may be had at the CUSTOM-HOUSE QUAY, and at

The General Steam Navigation Company's Offices,

56, Haymarket; Gilbert-street, two doors from Oxford-street; and 24, Crutched-friars.

CHARLES BESSELL, SECRETARY.

1826

The advertised domestic and continental sailing schedule for GSN 'from off the Custom-house or Tower' for the year 1826.

City of Edinburgh (1821) – the first steamship to travel between Edinburgh and London. [From a contemporary pen and ink drawing by William Edward Cooke]

London – the *City of Edinburgh* – was commissioned in 1821; she was owned by the London & Edinburgh Steam Packet Company, and was soon joined by the *Mountaineer*. Neither vessel was in service during the winter months when services were curtailed.

A competitor appeared on the Edinburgh route in 1824 when GSN chartered the steamer *Soho* to run an 'express' service from London to Edinburgh. Both services were centred on Brewer's Quay and loaded and unloaded passengers anchored in the Pool off Custom House Quay by boat. For a while the London and Edinburgh-based factions vied with each other, bringing out ever-faster and more reliable wooden paddle steamers – each more comfortably fitted out and better-suited for the carriage of passengers. At first the steamers were erratic and undependable with overcomplicated engines. For a time the sailing schooners retained the edge except when the weather was unfavourable, but, as the steamers and the services became more robust during the 1820s, so competition between the steamers intensified.

The inaugural steam sailing by the *Queen of Scotland*, between Aberdeen and London, took place in 1827. Her London agent was Messrs Smith & Sons of Galley Quay, described in advertisements as 'the second above Tower Stairs'. On her first voyage south she carried a cargo of 210 cattle and 700 boxes of salmon. The first iron-hulled vessel on the service was the *City of London*, which was commissioned in 1844.

Still looking very much the paddle-assisted sailing ship, the Aberdeen to London packet *City of London* (1844) was the first iron-hulled vessel built for the Aberdeen Steam Navigation Company. [*The Illustrated London News*]

But there was still considerable resentment on the river for the pioneer steamships. Cope Cornford wrote in *A Century of Sea Trading*:

> The watermen and lightermen used to pull their boats right across the bows of steamships, and then lie on their oars. When they were cut down, as they frequently were, they accused the steamship companies of running them down on purpose. It was out in evidence before the Select Committee of 1831, that a lighterman lashed two barges stem to stern and placed them across the fairway in the path of an approaching steamship; and that a wrathful bargeman, his craft under sail, steered straight into a steamship uttering the strange cry 'I will make your wheel clatter!'.

The outcome of the Select Committee helped neither the concerns of the watermen nor those of the steamship owners. Indeed the issues could only be resolved several years later when the watermen themselves embraced the new technology. In the meantime, both the travelling public and the shippers accepted the steamship and admired its ability to maintain advertised schedules. The pioneer steamships based in the Pool had done their job, and the new technology had become established.

The first steam paddle tugs to work in the Pool, and for that matter on the Thames, were the *Lady Dundas*, which arrived from the Tyne in 1832, and the *Wear*, which followed shortly afterwards from Sunderland. The primary role of the tugs was to help the sailing colliers manoeuvre in the Pool and assist them in getting to and from their anchorages, ready to discharge cargoes of coal. The *Wear* demonstrated the need for power as she was incapable of keeping her head to the tide in the river, let alone assisting another vessel. Having noted this, the newly formed London-based tug company William Watkins commissioned its first paddle tug, the *Monarch*, in 1833. Frank Burtt wrote of her:

> The *Monarch* hailed from the north. Built of wood and nearly 65 feet in length, 14 feet beam and a draught of 7 feet 5 inches. She was clincher built, having a cut-away bow and counter stern. Tonnage just over 26. The engine registered just over 20 Nominal HP being built by Wait of North Shields.

The little steamship was a great success in her role with the sailing colliers. She was reboilered in 1845, given new paddle wheels in 1856, reboilered again five years later, and only sold for demolition in 1876. Her final sale price realised a princely £40. In her early days, before she was reboilered for the first time, she ate coal at a great rate, and it was not uncommon for her to 'borrow' coal from her tow!

It was not until the 1840s that steam tugs were built of larger dimensions with more powerful engines for use in the Thames for ship handling and in the estuary. By 1848 it is recorded that there were thirty-three steam tugs working in the Thames, both handling the sailing colliers and the larger ships that were coming up to the Pool of London. Nine belonged to the Caledonian Steam Towing Company, eight to the Shipowners Towing Company, eight to the Thames Steam Towing Company, four to Thomas Petley, and four to William Watkins. However, the discovery of gold in Australia brought a flurry of new and second-hand tugs to London in order to help avoid delays in the passenger ship departures for the Antipodes!

The larger tugs went out to seek becalmed sailing ships in order to contract payment for towing them up-river to the Pool. Typical of these was Watkins' famous paddle tug

William Watkins' *Uncle Sam* (1849) was typical of the early wooden-hulled tugs on the Thames, complete with bowsprit and twin funnels placed abaft.

Uncle Sam, built at West Ham in 1849. These pioneer tugs were the start of a major industry on the Thames, with tugs large and small designed for handling the larger ships in the docks and, at the smaller end of the scale, for towing barges loaded in the docks to destinations in the Pool and up-river. The first iron-hulled tug on the Thames was the paddler *Friends to all Nations*, built in Newcastle in 1851 for Thomas Petley of London.

The screw tug was slow in coming on the river, as P. N. Thomas described in *British Steam Tugs*:

> Although Captain John Ericsson built the screw tug *Francis B Ogden* at Wapping in 1837 and with her proved the effectiveness of the screw propeller for towing, the tug owners of London ignored him. Ericsson was not put out and made a second attempt with his *Robert F Stockton*, this time towing coal lighters, but again he met with the same lack of interest… The first operational screw tug on the Thames seems to have been the *Magnet* (1854) owned first by Wm. Hughes and then by James Thomas who followed with the *Jackall* (1856).

The sailing collier was doomed with the arrival of the *John Bowes* – an iron-hulled screw driven collier, built on the Tyne by Palmers of Jarrow in 1852. She was designed to improve efficiency in carrying the coal down from north-east England as the railways had already started bringing coal at competitive prices from the Midland Coalfield to London. The *John Bowes* was just 437 gross registered tons and had a sea speed of 8 knots. Her twin-cylinder steam engine was placed well aft in her iron hull, and it drove a single screw propeller.

On her maiden voyage she carried 540 tons of coal – more than twice the load of the traditional sailing ship – from Sunderland to the Colliers Dock in just 48 hours. The *John Bowes* was able to perform a round trip from the Tyne to London in ten days. Much of this time, however, was spent in the East & West India Colliers Dock discharging her cargo; not surprising then that the *John Bowes* was withdrawn from the coal trade within a year and put onto a new parcel service between the Pool and Newcastle, in competition with the established steamer service already operated by GSN. Nevertheless, the obvious success of the steam-driven screw collier in terms of efficiency of operation, despite tide and wind, was taken on board by the colliery owners in the north-east and it was not long before the sailing collier was ousted from the North Sea. Indeed, Palmers built twenty-five more colliers with an aggregate 12,210 gross registered tons, to a slightly larger and more powerful specification than the *John Bowes*, in the two years between 1852 and 1854.

The first iron-hulled vessel to sail regularly overseas from the Pool was the GSN paddle steamer *Rainbow*, commissioned in 1837 and used by the company to investigate the performance of the new technology. The pioneer vessel was also the centre of Admiralty attention, while their Lordships oversaw experiments to validate the magnetic compass aboard an otherwise magnetic ship. *Rainbow* was then placed on the Antwerp and Rotterdam services from the company's newly acquired St Katherine's Wharf. The next iron-hulled ship was the *Magician* in 1844, later to be deployed at Newhaven, and was followed in 1845 by the *Triton*. Thereafter, only iron-hulled (and later steel-hulled) vessels were ordered by GSN, although a number of wooden-hulled paddlers subsequently joined the company as second-hand purchases.

Many of the pioneer long-distance sailings, such as the voyages of the wooden-hulled steamship *William Fawcett* into the Mediterranean for the embryonic P&O company in 1835, did not start in the Pool. These ships tended to load and unload at Blackwall using the facilities of the East India Company, some also at Deptford. Nevertheless, sailing hoys were used to tranship cargoes from the East India Dock and the riverside wharves at Blackwall, and many of these sailed up-river into the Pool to discharge. The Pool, at this time, was grossly overcrowded, with sailing colliers moored four deep along its shores and anchored across the river, leaving little spare capacity for sailings by pioneer steamships.

The wooden-hulled paddle steamer on the long-haul journeys was soon over taken by the lighter structures of the iron hull. The Royal Mail Line introduced its revolutionary iron-hulled paddle steamer *Atrato* to its West Indies service from London in 1857. The new breed of ship soon demonstrated the benefits of the design and of the fire-resistant material she was constructed of; however, it was not long before even she was superseded by the iron-hulled screw steamer, giving the benefit of a fully submerged driving propeller rather than paddle wheels that dipped into and out of the water as the ship rolled. The first commercial screw steamer was the *Novelty*, a larger successor to Henry Wimshurst's first screw steamship, the *Archimedes*. The *Novelty* plied between Blackwall and Constantinople, with a service speed of 7 knots, if only for a brief period in 1840.

The *Atrato* (1857) was typical of the early iron-hulled paddle steamers designed for long-distance services – owned by the Royal Mail Steam Packet Company, she served between London, Plymouth, and the West Indies.

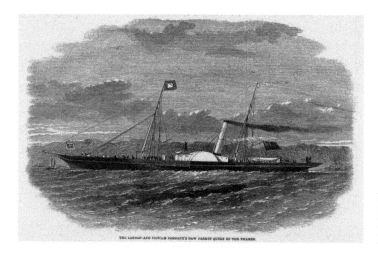

Queen of the Thames (1861) from *The Illustrated London News* 1861.

The dining saloon aboard the *Queen of the Thames* (1861) from a wood engraving by G. Durand, published in *The Graphic*.

Pioneer steamships using the Pool, however, were many, with each successive generation of steamer outweighing the benefits of its predecessor. Progress developed through the simple steam engine to the compound engine and eventually to the triple expansion steam engine, while hull construction went through various developments from the wooden hull to the iron hull and later to the even lighter steel hull. As all these innovations were introduced, they were quickly seen in the Pool.

Of the Thames passenger services, steamers such as *Queen of the Thames* with its massive dining saloon below the main deck were extremely popular. However, the greatest innovation was the arrival of the pioneer saloon steamer *Alexandra*, as described by Frank Burtt:

The *Alexandra* was built in 1865 and originally intended as a blockade runner, but the American Civil War having ended before she was completed she was purchased by a concern known as The Saloon Steam Packet Company of London, and became the first large steam boat of the saloon type employed in passenger traffic on the River Thames between London Bridge and Gravesend. At the time she was advertised to carry 1,048 passengers which 'can be distributed that there be no apprehension of over-crowding. She is substantially built, and her fitments and decorations are ingenious and tasteful without being unnecessarily costly, while the general arrangements for her management are such as will secure the favour of the public.'

From then on the flush-decked Thames passenger paddle steamer was in disfavour with the public, who now preferred the all-weather facilities offered by the saloon steamer. Pioneers continued to appear in the Pool through the remainder of the nineteenth and the first half of the twentieth century. Steam, of course, was then overtaken by the oil engine – the motor ship, again with pioneer ships, setting the standards. Innovation continues today with the modern and futuristic, fast and environmentally friendly river boat services that are currently being introduced in service on the river for the benefit of commuters and tourists alike. These ships are specially designed for the tidal conditions on the river and the hull shape is configured to minimise wash that could upset other river users.

The barges or lighters were distinctive to the Thames, as P. N. Thomas described:

In the docks the ship' cargoes were transferred into sailing barges which distributed them down river or into lighters which carried the goods up the river. The lighters had no means of propulsion but, riding on the flow of the tidal currents, they were rowed by the lightermen with a huge sweep or oar. 'Driving' was an art which has been passed on through an apprenticeship system. The art lies, not only in the lighterman's ability to drive, but also in his intimate knowledge of the river and its tidal forces, for he relies on its assistance to cover long distances from the lower reaches of the river to the wharves upstream and back...

The Thames lighter has a 'swim' bow, i.e. the bow rakes heavily forward and the tug usually tows its lighters on a very short line with the stem of the lighter hard up against and overhanging her stern. This caused for considerable tumblehome aft [the upper part of the hull and bulwarks leaned in towards the ship] to avoid damage, but despite this... it was quite usual to sheath the stern bulwarks with oak to protect the iron sheeting. The same tumblehome is required all round the tug as she often had to force her way into a tier of lighters to pick out the one which she has to tow...

Just after 1860 the towage of lighters really got underway and for economy's sake they were formed into 'trains'. This was not over popular with the other users of the river who saw the 'trains' as an obstruction to the free passage of vessels. The lighters were towed in groups up to a limit of six, and these were arranged in pairs or three abreast in the case of the narrower beamed lighters which were used upstream and which had provision for a rudder. The overall length of the tow from the stern of the tug to the stern of the aftermost lighter was restricted to 320 feet [in the Pool]... It was apparent from early accident reports that the tugs did not always tow with the lighters hard up against the stern and that many collisions were caused by lighters on a long tow line veering about the river if the tug was forced to make a sudden alteration of course because of other traffic.

Chapter 6

Coasting Passenger Trades

The steamer slowly began to dominate the east coast passenger trade and numerous companies were formed to operate new steamship services following the earlier success of those on the Leith and Aberdeen routes (Chapter 5). New companies included, for example, the Aberdeen & London Shipping Company, Humber Union Company, and the Dundee & Hull Steam Packet Company. They all used London agents based in the Pool but were able to berth alongside only for loading and unloading, with passengers brought out to the ships at anchor by the watermen.

The development of the longer west coast services south from the Clyde, via Liverpool, Bristol, Plymouth, Portsmouth, and eventually to London, evolved in quite a different way to the east coast services. The first routes were from Belfast and Dublin to London with intermediate calls at a variety of ports including Plymouth, Cowes and Portsmouth. The British & Irish Steam Packet Company was formed in 1836 with the wooden paddlers *City of Limerick*, *Devonshire*, and *Shannon* to maintain the Dublin to London service. In 1831 the Saint George Steam Packet Company put the 201-ton *Lee*, built at Chester in 1825, onto a new and prestigious service between Liverpool and London with calls at Cork, Plymouth, Exeter, and Cowes. Once established, the route was then maintained by the *Earl of Roden* and the brand-new *Victory*. The pioneering Saint George company was restructured in 1843 when it became the City of Cork Steamship Company. In due course fierce competition developed on the Dublin route with three companies – City of Dublin, City of Cork, and the Waterford companies – all vying for trade by the middle of the century.

The Irish ships had regular weekly departures from London Dublin Steam Wharf for Cowes, Plymouth, Falmouth and Dublin by the *Shannon* and *Thames* and the older steamer *City of Dublin* of the Dublin and London Steam Packet Company. Fares from London to Plymouth were £1 3s 6d in the cabin, 17s in the second cabin, and 5s for the deck, and nearly as much again for the journey from Plymouth to Dublin. The City of Dublin Steam Company also ran a service between London and Yarmouth with the paddle steamers *Mersey* and later the *Hibernia*. However, the Norfolk route was taken over in 1838 by GSN who put *Sir Edward Banks* on the service, with Irongate Wharf as the London terminal, and joined in 1839 by *Ramona* with London departures on Tuesdays and Saturdays.

In 1832 the East India Company opened the Brunswick Wharf on the south bank of the Pool below St Katherine Dock. This was designed as a transhipment point for the sailing hoys serving the East India fleet berthed at Blackwall and at the East India Dock. It also became the home of the London & Edinburgh Steam Packet Company and several of the GSNC domestic services, including the Edinburgh route.

The Dundee & Perth Shipping Company commissioned its first wooden paddler *Dundee*, and then her counterpart *Perth*, in 1833 and 1834 respectively. Described at the time as the fastest and best-appointed on the east coast, the Dundee company delighted in overtaking rivals from the Edinburgh and Aberdeen stations. The service was discontinued in the winter months when the vessels were laid up.

The GSN Edinburgh service was supplemented in 1837 by the *Leith*, the largest vessel in the fleet to date and built appropriately at Leith 'for the purpose of conciliating the feelings and opinions of those among whom to a considerable extent the influence of the company [GSN] was comparatively unknown'.

On the west coast the Thames & Clyde Screw Shipping Company's *Metropolitan* started on a regular run between Glasgow and London, joined by the *Cosmopolitan* in April 1852 when a weekly service commenced. Although the sisters did not carry passengers, the *Metropolitan* was celebrated when, in November 1851, she broke all records with a passage south – arriving at Wapping just three days after leaving Greenock.

The Carron Company, without any earlier investment in paddle steamers, started to change from sail to steam in the early 1850s. However, passenger-carrying had been discontinued on the sloops in the 1820s, although deck passengers were occasionally carried. The cargo fleet was expanded in the 1860s and 1870s; the Victorian demand for iron fireplaces and bath tubs from the Carron Company iron works was insatiable.

At Leith, the Edinburgh company also forsook its schooners and turned to steam. Never having owned paddle steamers, the company's first steamship was the 506 tons gross iron-hulled screw vessel *Prompt*, which was delivered from Barclay & Curle's yard on the Clyde in 1853. A second generation of steamers offered far more creature comforts to passengers. In 1861 and 1862 three new ships were delivered to company specifications – the *Oscar*, *Fingal*, and *Morna* – with a further trio in 1865 and 1866, comprising the *Staffa*, *Malvina*, and *Iona*. This was a modern fleet designed to overshadow competing companies.

Further north, the Aberdeen – London service, now based at Wapping, saw a period of intense competition with the introduction of iron screw steamers. The Northern Steam Company operated two screw steamers and competed with the Aberdeen company paddlers from 1860, but the interests were merged in 1861.

Tragically, the flagship, *City of Aberdeen*, was wrecked near her home port in January 1871 and replaced by a new ship of the same name, costing £40,000, in the spring of 1873. The Aberdeen company had arrived in the new era. With return fares of £1 10s First Class and 15s Second, plus 15s and 10s respectively for a steward and full provisions, the cost of travel was actually cheaper than it had been in the early days of the paddle steamer when the return cabin fare was £5.

In 1875 the Aberdeen company acquired its own wharf and warehousing at Limehouse – a facility it retained until it was taken over by the Coast Lines group in 1945. Shortly afterwards it took delivery of its own screw passenger tug, *Ich Dien,* which was used to take passengers to and from Westminster Pier in connection with arrivals and departures at Limehouse. On 23 August 1879 the *City of London* was run down and sunk by the German steamer *Vesta,* shortly after sailing from the wharf at Limehouse. She was later raised and repaired, but the incident serves to remind of the dangers of navigating the crowded River Thames.

The Dundee, Perth & London Company upgraded to screw steamers from 1853. By the early 1860s the London to Dundee service was operated by the *London, Scotia* and *Anglia.*

The Carron Line commissioned the magnificent sisters *Forth* and *Thames* in 1887 to reintroduce passenger-carrying between Carron Wharf at Wapping and Carron Dock at Grangemouth. The ships offered sixty-five First Class and thirty saloon class berths for the 30-hour passage to London. The new passenger service was second to none and offered serious competition to the established passenger services from nearby Leith and even Dundee. The two mainline passenger ships were joined by a third, the *Grange* in 1892, and a fourth, the two-funnelled *Avon* in 1897. The *Avon* also had twin-screws – a unique feature in the coasting trades – and offered ninety-five First Class berths and fifty-two Second Class, plus space for up to 215 deck passengers. She made the trip between London and Grangemouth in just 28 hours. Single fares were 22s First Class, 16s Second Class, and 10s deck.

The Edinburgh company also had a modern fleet operating its London service. By 1890 the eldest ship was the *Marmion* dating from 1871, but nevertheless offering comfortable accommodation in two classes – equal with the Carron ships in every way but speed. Fleet mates were the *Malvina, Meteor,* and *Iona,* of which the *Meteor* was

The passenger tug *Ich Dien* (1877) on one of her trips between Limehouse and Westminster Pier, conveying passengers to and from the Aberdeen steamer.

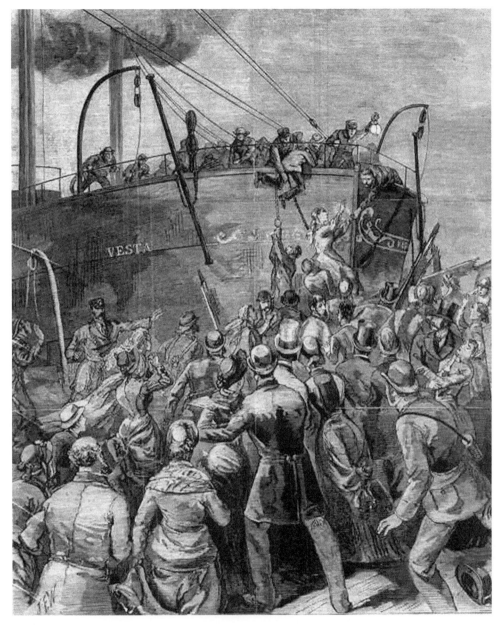

The rescue of passengers from the deck of the *City of London* after the collision with the *Vesta* on 13 August 1879. [*The Pictorial World*]

the youngest vessel, having been completed only in 1887. The *Malvina* and *Marmion* were replaced by two attractive quasi-sisters, respectively the *Fingal* in 1894 and the *Fiona* in 1905.

Bigger and better steamers were also built for the Aberdeen company, notably the *Hogarth* in 1893, which was built at the local yard of Hall, Russell & Company for

The Carron Company's magnificent steamer *Avon* (1897) setting off down the Thames after her evening departure from Carron Wharf, destined for Grangemouth.

The Edinburgh steamer *Fingal* (1894) in the Lower Pool on departure from St Katherine's Wharf.

£37,600. She worked the London service alongside the *Ban-Righ*, with the slightly younger vessels *City of London* and *City of Aberdeen* kept in reserve.

The Dundee company commissioned the fourth *Dundee* when she was delivered by Gourlay Brothers of Dundee in 1885. First Class accommodation was moved from the traditional poop housing and placed amidships, offering sixty-five berths. This reflected confidence in a smoother-running and better-balanced engine, as she was equipped with the brand-new triple expansion system rather than the compound engine of her earlier fleet mates. The poop now housed a further sixty berths for Second Class, and she was licensed to carry an additional seventy-five deck passengers. The ship was fitted throughout with low-voltage direct current electricity and she offered a clean pair of heels with a cruising speed of 15 knots. The new *Dundee* was a major success and in 1890 was followed by the *Perth*, and in 1892 the *London*. Both were somewhat larger, but built broadly along the same lines as the *Dundee*, and with accommodation for 350 passengers.

The London-based GSN operating from Irongate Wharf in the Pool to Edinburgh maintained the *Rainbow* and *Osprey* in service, dating from 1872 and 1877 respectively. Other vessels were drafted in from time to time from the company's Continental and Mediterranean services, notably the *Gannet* and *Lapwing* – both completed in 1879 – as demand required.

So what was the journey between the Scottish ports and London actually like at the close of the nineteenth century? Breakfast was served at 9 a.m., 'dinner' at 2 p.m., and 'tea' at 7 p.m. A typical First Class breakfast menu aboard the *City of London* was equal to anything ashore and offered fresh herring, fried sole, fried cod, boiled eggs, mutton chops, beefsteak, fried sausages, grilled bacon, stewed kidneys, American dry hash, and cold meats. At sea the master, Captain Chambers, presided over all meals, resplendent in his gold braid and full blue serge uniform. The dinner menu included beef, mutton, lamb, duck, fowl, and ox tongue, with accompanying cauliflower and green peas.

As the day ended, the First Class passengers opted for one of three choices; comforting tumblers of 'Special Scotch' were on offer in the smoke room on the promenade deck, while in the deck saloon, with its comfy sofas, fervent hymn-singing took place to the accompaniment of a resident pianist, and the poop became a focus for smokers watching the patent log revolve on its wire as the ship surged forward.

Life aboard the coastal liners in late Victorian Second Class accommodation was not quite as sumptuous. Nevertheless, contemporary accounts describe wholesome, if comparatively plain, meals being available, with porter and other beverages offered at shore-side prices. Deck passengers obviously had to sit it out in the saloon but Second Class berths, largely segregated male and female dormitory-style berths, provided clean and safe accommodation, albeit somewhat spartan. Bedding was not provided for Second Class passengers and they were reminded to bring a blanket for the voyage.

Passenger routes from a variety of English east coast ports to London were also well developed. There were important passenger links with the capital from Newcastle, Middlesbrough and Sunderland. The main Newcastle service was

Advertisement for the steamers *Sentinel* (1860) and *Brigadier* (1855) running to Irongate Wharf from the Tyne in 1863.

provided by the Tyne Steam Shipping Company, which was a joint stock company formed in 1864 in order to consolidate various local services to London and the continent, including William Stephens' service to the Irongate Wharf in the Pool with the *Sentinel* and *Brigadier*. All the steamers were screw-propelled – the earlier ones being iron-hulled rather than steel. The London service was initially operated by the *Otter* and the first *Earl Percy*, but most vessels were interchangeable, with some London calls made en route to Dunkirk. Losses were significant, with the first *Earl Percy* being wrecked off Tynemouth during the second year of the new company's existence; she was replaced by a new purpose-built steamer for the London route, which was given the same name. The new *Earl Percy* was a great favourite with the travelling public, but in 1888 she too was wrecked, this time on Whitby rocks.

James Layton writes in the World Ship Society Teesside Branch journal:

In 1858 the fares to London aboard the *Brigadier* were 15/- (22/6 return), 10/- (15/- return) and sailors as deck passengers 7/-. By 1876 the fares had been reduced to 13/6 (21/- return), 8/6 (13/- return) and 5/- on deck. After 1891 they were 12/- (18/- return) and 8/- (12/- return). The fares from Middlesbrough to London remained unchanged from 1863 until 1903 at 11/6 (17/6 return) for First Class passengers and 7/6 (11/6 return) for Second Class. When the Tyne-Tees company was created in 1903 the

Middlesbrough to London fares were increased by 6 pence to bring them into line with the Newcastle fares.

The Middlesbrough passenger route was greatly improved by the introduction of the *Dione* in 1863 under the ownership of the London & Middlesbrough Steamship Company, which in 1880 became part of the Tees Union Shipping Company. The *Dione* stayed on this service until finally sold by the Tyne-Tees Steam Shipping Company in 1908 following the amalgamation of the Tyne and Tees interests in 1903. The various north-east England sailings from London focused on the Free Trade Wharf, which was created in 1884 jointly by the Tees interests. The Free Trade Wharf Company also acted as London agents for other shipping companies, which also included a number of coasting companies such as George Bazeley & Company of Penzance. This wharf had one time belonged to the East India Company and was situated at Ratcliff, just one mile downstream from the Tower of London on the north bank. The Sunderland boat, the *General Havelock*, owned by R. M. Hudson and his Havelock Line, berthed at Wapping Basin outside London Dock.

The biggest ship to be built for the Tyne company was the *Royal Dane*, and as her name suggests she was designed to inaugurate a new route to Copenhagen. She was built in 1874 by J. W. Richards & Company at Walker and cost £34,957. However, competition on the new route became intense and the Tyne Steam Shipping Company withdrew in 1877, and placed its flagship on the London service. By 1884 all the passenger steamers were equipped with low-voltage electric lighting and each ship carried the mandatory piano in the saloon and even had small libraries available to the passengers.

A new ship, the *Tynesider*, had her engines aft, with accommodation-amidships and was of similar capacity to the *Royal Dane*, but altogether more powerful and consequently able to complete the passage time a few hours quicker. The slightly larger sister, the *Londoner*, was delivered in 1891. Both the *Londoner* and *Tynesider* could accommodate about 200 berthed and unberthed passengers. Sadly, the *Londoner* was lost in collision off the Happisburgh Light in 1893 and the *Royal Dane* was hastily drafted back onto the route. The *New Londoner* was ordered to replace the lost ship.

The Middlesbrough route, operated by the Tees Union Shipping Company, was also popular. By the end of the century the service was maintained by the steamers *Claudia*, completed only in 1878, and *Dione*. There were also passenger berths available on the Hartlepool to London service introduced by Furness Withy in 1888, when the passenger steamers *Buccaneer* (built in 1890 and acquired in 1902) and the purpose-built *New Oporto* (completed in 1903) came into service. Furness Withy amalgamated the ships and their interest in the coastal route with the newly formed Tyne-Tees Steam Shipping Company shortly afterwards to give them a seventh share of the new company.

The *General Havelock*, dating from 1868, maintained the Sunderland to London passenger and cargo route for R. M. Hudson. The steamer stopped off Scarborough during the summer months where she was attended to by the company tender *Comet*. The service was well patronised, particularly in the warmer (and calmer) months, and was effectively a one-ship monopoly on the route to London.

The *Tynesider* (1888) on her evening departure from Free Trade Wharf bound for Newcastle. [Harold Appleyard collection]

The Clyde Shipping Company steamer *Tuskar* (1890) working cargo in St Katherine Dock.

Sailings by the Clyde Shipping Company from Glasgow to St Katherine Dock at London commenced in 1882. Calls were made at Belfast, Plymouth, Southampton, Newhaven, and Sussex, and a host of new ships were built and commissioned. A notable group was formed by the identical twins *Cumbrae* and *Toward*, and the slightly smaller and slower *Cloch*, which were all delivered in 1883. The prototype steel-hulled *Fastnet* was followed by a further eight iron-hulled ships before the next steel-hulled vessel was delivered, the *Inishtrahull*, in 1885; even then a mix of iron and steel ships entered the company fleet until the last iron-hulls, *Sanda* and *Dungeness*, were delivered in 1892. The *Inishtrahull* was the first vessel to be equipped with a triple expansion engine. Further new ships were commissioned and at the end of the nineteenth century there were four sailings a week between Glasgow and London – two of which sailed via Belfast.

A period of intense competition on the Dublin to London route eventually left the British & Irish Steam Packet Company in sole charge, with a five ship fleet serving London. Malcolm McRonald in his book *The Irish Boats: Volume 1* summarises the conditions aboard ship:

> The ships all had berths for around 120 saloon and 50 second cabin passengers, and also carried unberthed steerage passengers. There was a full complement of stewards and stewardesses. The service was fashionable and a piano was put on board each ship during the summer. The ships' normal speed was 13 knots. They also operated cruises from Dublin, usually to Falmouth and Plymouth...

On the west coast routes from Liverpool, F. H. Powell & Company and Samuel Hough were initially competitors. Eventually, in 1913, they amalgamated their services, many of which had become shared routes to form Powell, Bacon & Hough Lines and in due course rebranded as Coast Lines. Of the better known Powell ships, the *Faithful* joined the company in 1871 and the *Graceful* was acquired in 1893 from the Union Steamship Company. The Powell departures were offered each week from London, Regents Canal Dock, and Liverpool by the 1880s in collaboration with Samuel Hough, terminating at the Regent's Canal Wharf on the Thames. The fare from London to Liverpool was 25s, meals extra: breakfast 2s, lunch 2s 6d and tea 2s – the latter a cooked 'high tea', there being no such thing as a late dinner in Victorian times. The Powell funnel colours were, of course, black with a white chevron and were passed on in due course to the Coast Lines Group.

This vast array of coastal passenger and cargo liners all used the Pool as their London terminal. The fares were competitive against those offered by the railway companies and the services provided an attractive alternative to the routine of train travel. This was not to last, as passengers eventually took to the increasingly faster rail connections and later still took to road transport when it became a viable option. In consequence, cargo-only steamers were introduced that slowly replaced those with passenger accommodation, but all this was to happen in the twentieth century.

The Powell Line steamer *Graceful* (1886) on passage from Liverpool, having departed from the Regents Canal Basin.

The coastal passenger liner trade slowly gave way to cargo ships; the GSN cargo steamer *Falcon* (1927) seen at Butler's Wharf in the early 1950s. [Pan American World Airways System Photographic Section, New York]

Chapter 7

Twentieth Century Coastal Passenger Liners

All the coasting companies enjoyed the heydays of the 1900s. There were excellent cargo loadings and high passenger numbers were boosted by round trip passengers from the provinces. With the Victorian constraints finally lifted, the Georgian era was a time of excess, and the seasonal summer passenger numbers swelled on all the domestic sea routes to the capital. Robins wrote in *Coastal Passenger Liners of the British Isles*:

> The halcyon years before the Great War were the boom years of the coastal passenger liners. The dockers' and lightermens' strikes had gone away. Maritime safety had greatly improved, particularly in the light of the *Titanic* disaster in 1912, subsequent to which passenger ships were required to carry additional lifesaving equipment. Industry was providing cargoes, and some passengers had both time and money available to spend on a week-long coastal cruise and could arrange business appointments in the capital before the return voyage, while others merely took advantage of the competitive fares that were on offer. This was an idyll that all the coastal liner operators would remember before the awful dawning of the Great War began to overwhelm Britain, her people and her ships.

The Tyne Steam Shipping Company was merged in October 1903, along with the smaller Tees Union Shipping Company, its four steamers, and its subsidiary the Free Trade Wharf Company of London. The Tyne-Tees Steam Shipping Company was thus formed with the incorporation of the coastal ships of Furness Withy on their London to Hartlepool feeder service. Furness Withy had operated the passenger and cargo steamers *New Oporto* and *Buccaneer* to the capital and offered a small number of berths for passengers.

The newly formed Tyne-Tees Steam Shipping Company owned a diverse fleet, including several old units such as the *John Ormston* dating from 1873 and the *Royal Dane* from 1875. The Middlesbrough and Stockton passenger service to the company-owned Free Trade Wharf at London was maintained by the *Claudia* and

'Powell Line, Liverpool and London Steamers': the *Powerful* (1903) on the approaches to the Thames Estuary.

the venerable *Dione*, which dated from 1868, while the Newcastle to London route was in the hands of the *New Londoner* and *Tynesider*.

On the west coast, F. H. Powell & Company, the Powell Line, introduced two new and very popular passenger and cargo ships to the Liverpool to London route – the *Powerful*, built in 1903, and the *Masterful*, built two years later. They were the largest ships in the fleet at 1,607 and 1,794 tons gross respectively; the *Masterful* capable of 12 knots and her older sister 13 knots. Principally cargo ships, the *Powerful* offered First Class accommodation for fifty passengers wanting to enjoy the cruise element of the voyage, while the *Masterful* could accommodate eighty. The *Powerful* sailed from London on Wednesdays and the *Masterful* on Saturdays. This pair set a reputation for speed, comfort and regularity that was unequalled, or so their timetable claimed.

The magnificent new 1,932 tons gross steamer *Samuel Hough* was the first of the Samuel Hough Limited second-generation steamers; she was commissioned in 1905, ready to take up her roster on the west coast passenger trade. The Hough vision peaked with the delivery in 1911 of a consort for the *Samuel Hough* – the *Dorothy Hough*. The *Dorothy Hough* was magnificently adorned with a grey-painted hull and dark brown upperworks. She had luxurious accommodation for passengers who were accommodated on the main deck amidships (more could be carried in the height of season on sofa beds in the main lounge), the dining saloon was forward on the main deck beneath the smoking room, and off this was a small cabin for ladies – both public spaces being housed on the upper deck beneath the wheelhouse.

The *Dorothy Hough* was the ultimate in design of the west coast passenger cargo liners, but she was not allowed to keep her name for long. In 1913 Powell, Bacon & Hough Lines was created out of the three separate coasting companies at Liverpool to form what would later become Coast Lines. F. H. Powell & Company was the dominant partner, and the ships adopted their 'coast' nomenclature and later the classic Powell black funnel with a white chevron as the new corporate image. Shortly afterwards the *Dorothy Hough* was given the corporate name *Southern Coast*, and the *Powerful* was renamed *Eastern Coast*.

A twice-weekly express cargo service was operated by Fisher, Renwick & Company between Manchester and London. Only when purpose-built tonnage was built for the route could the numerous earlier enquiries for passenger berths be satisfied; the sisters *Carbineer* and *Musketeer* were delivered from the Tyne in 1907 and 1908 respectively and each offered berths for up to eight passengers in the summer season. They were handsome looking ships with a tall black funnel adorned by three thin white stripes. Passenger demand soon outstripped availability, so when the *Lancer* was commissioned in 1909 she too offered a few berths, as did the *Cuirassier,* which first arrived at London in 1914. The final passenger ship to be built for Fisher, Renwick was the *Halburdier*, delivered in 1915, but sadly she never enjoyed fare-paying passengers and was sunk by an enemy torpedo off Bardsey Island on 6 January 1918. Passenger berths were not offered after the First World War, most of the passenger carrying units having been lost during the hostilities.

The Clyde Shipping Company started the new century with seven virtually brand-new passenger cargo steamers on their Glasgow to Ireland and south coast of England to

The Clyde Shipping Company's steamer *Rathlin* (1905) making a stately approach up the Thames on her way up to St Katherine Dock. [Nautical Photo Agency]

St Katherine Dock routes. Despite this fleet of modern steamers, the company continued its ongoing fleet replacement with the delivery of three broadly similar passenger and cargo steamers between 1903 and 1907. They were the near sisters *Sheerness*, *Rathlin* and a new *Pladda*. A fourth ship, the *Aranmore*, was completed without any passenger accommodation. These vessels each had tall and thin funnels with an open bridge over the captain's cabin. The first pair had four lifeboats amidships, whereas the boats were split between the poop and the central accommodation structure aboard the *Pladda*.

In 1911, two rather special sister ships were delivered from the Caledon Shipbuilding & Engineering Company at Dundee – the *Ballycotton* and the *Warner*. These were the first steamers to have all the passengers' accommodation situated amidships, reflecting confidence in the smooth running of the triple expansion engine that was then standard.

At Cork the substantial and well-appointed steamers *Killarney* and *Blarney* maintained the year-round service between Cork and London. A twice-weekly service was offered at the height of the summer season and at other holiday periods. When the new steamer *Lismore* joined the City of Cork Steam Packet Company in 1905, she too was occasionally rostered on London duties, as also were the *Ardmore* and *Bandon*, delivered in 1909 and 1910 respectively.

At Penzance, George Bazeley & Sons thrived with four ships providing a twice-weekly service between London and Bristol for passengers and general cargo using the passenger cargo steamers *Cloch*, *Coath*, and *Mercutio*, as well as the smaller *Gervase*. They were joined in 1907 by William Sloan's *Solway*, which replaced the *Gervase*. G. W. Tripp recalls a passage from London to Penzance in an article that first appeared in *Sea Breezes*, October 1955:

> The writer well remembers boarding the steamer *Coath*, of the Little Western Steamship Company, at Free Trade Wharf in 1908, to travel to Penzance, after which the vessel proceeded to Bristol. It is hardly accurate to say that the voyage was made to Penzance, as when Captain Spray stated that he had an exceptionally heavy cargo and was also putting into Dartmouth, a decision was made to leave the ship at Torquay, the first port of call, take the train to Totnes, and proceed thence by steamer down the beautiful Dart to Dartmouth, where the *Coath* was rejoined – a very pleasant diversion.

Coast Lines sought to buy out other coastal liner companies and in 1920 made an offer of £160,000 for Bazeley's business. In 1920 the business was transferred to Coast Lines, one steamer sold with the others given 'Coast' names. Administration moved to London, and Penzance was then served by calls from Coast Lines' steamers working on the company's longer routes. Other companies bought at that time included the British & Irish Steam Packet.

The London & Channel Islands Steamship Company was incorporated in 1899 after operating a cargo service for two years. The *Island Queen* and *May Queen* were commissioned with a handful of First Class passenger berths. Other ships were later commissioned with limited passenger accommodation, but demand for passenger berths was such that the *London Queen* was built in 1910 with as many as twenty berths, and the *Channel Queen* just two years later with forty berths. Departures were scheduled for Jersey and Guernsey twice a week from Eastern Dock at Shadwell until the company berth switched to Free Trade Wharf in the early 1950s. The next ship was the *Island Queen,* which was designed with sixty berths. However, she was delivered in 1916 and maintained the service only until requisitioned for war service in 1917, before being bought by the Admiralty. Passenger-carrying was not resumed after the First World War and the ships moved from the Lower Pool to a new berth in the India Docks.

After the First World War the Carron Line withdrew from passenger carrying after a short-lived revival. GSN still had the *Woodcock* running between Leith and London on a weekly circuit. She was replaced by a new ship of the same name in 1927 and followed by a second new ship, named *Woodlark,* in 1928. The new ships, like their predecessors, were registered at Leith rather than London, showing respect to their Scottish shipbuilders as well as potential Scottish clients – either passengers or shippers of goods. The new steamers were not sisters and had quite different cargo stowage,

The GSN tug *Gull* (1898) lying off Brewer's Wharf, summer 1932, ready to assist company ships or tow lighters to and from the ships. The Southern Railway steamer *Engadine* (1911) is seen moored below London Bridge ready for her daily excursion to the Nore Light.

GSN's *Cormorant* (1927) was one of a class of steamers designed to serve on any one of the domestic and foreign services operated by GSN, and is seen coming up the Thames to one of the many company wharves in the Pools.

but the pair offered comfortable accommodation in single and twin-berth cabins for twelve passengers. They normally offered twice-weekly departures from both Leith and Irongate Wharf at London. A number of ships were also built to serve both the domestic or European routes as required.

Following the short-lived depression of the early 1920s, passenger demand for the Leith to London service increased and the London & Edinburgh Shipping Company ordered a new passenger and cargo steamer; this was the magnificent *Royal Fusilier*. She had two and four berth cabins for 116 passengers and at peak times a further fourteen passengers could be berthed in the dining room, smoke room, and music room – the latter on the Bridge Deck. So successful was she, and so well received and supported by the travelling public, that within four years a quasi-sister was commissioned and given the name *Royal Archer*. The second new ship, built on the success of her consort, was even better appointed so that she immediately became the preferred option for travel. The ships often ran to capacity during the summer months in the late 1920s.

A smaller steamer, the *Royal Scot*, was commissioned in 1930. The new *Royal Scot* offered limited, although very much First Class accommodation for twelve passengers in two-berth cabins. The three-passenger-and-cargo-ship level of service between Leith and London was retained by the Edinburgh company throughout the 1930s.

The Dundee, Perth & London Shipping Company was able to resume passenger sailings to London only in July 1919 when its steamer *Arbroath* had been refurbished. She was replaced by the *Perth*, which was released by the Admiralty that summer ready for refit and refurbishment. The *Perth* had comfortable berths for 398 passengers in

The *Royal Fusilier* (1924) working cargo alongside the Hermitage Steam Wharf with the Carron Wharf upstream.

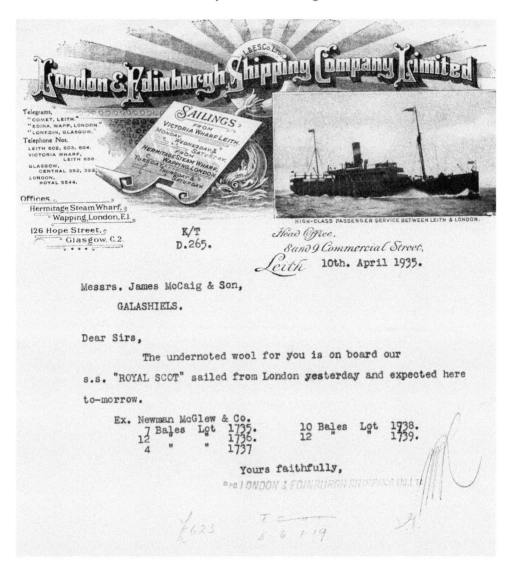

The day to day business of the London & Edinburgh Shipping Company: 'The undernoted wool for you is aboard our SS *Royal Scot*...'

addition to her thirty-seven crew (of which eight were seasonal catering staff aboard for the summer season only). There were sixty berths in First Class and a further ten for men in the smoking room and twelve for women in the music room. Second Class berths were divided between twenty-four in the poop, twenty in the stern sheets, fifty-two on the main deck, and an additional fourteen men (as a last resort) in the dining saloon.

The *London* joined the Dundee service after the war. She was capable of berthing thirty First Class passengers with Second Class in dormitory accommodation in the 'tween decks, reducing to only twelve First Class passengers out of season. The seasonal Second Class comprised awnings hung down the centre line to separate men and women with virtually no other comforts other than mattresses laid on the deck. In the early 1930s the Depression forced the big steamer *Perth* to lay up over winter, while a new twelve-passenger cargo steamer, the *Dundee*, was commissioned as her seasonal replacement.

Further north, at Aberdeen, the wartime hospital ship *Aberdonian* was returned to the Aberdeen Steam Navigation Company in May 1919. Her post-war passenger facilities were reduced to just eighty First Class and 120 Second and, following refurbishment work totalling nearly £22,000, she resumed her London sailings in the early autumn. The *City of London*, which had been chartered out for Leith to Iceland duties that summer under the Lauritzen flag, resumed duties also and a two-ship, twice-weekly service was commenced.

The Dundee steamer *London* (1921) inbound to the Lower Pool, having dropped some of her passengers at Southend Pier. [From an oil painting by Derrick Smoothy]

The Aberdeen steamer *Aberdonian* (1909) in the Thames with an Ellerman liner beyond her. The Aberdeen steamers berthed at Limehouse and later moved to Free Trade Wharf.

The Aberdeen company suffered very badly at the hands of the London dockers, whose sudden and repeated strike actions played havoc with passenger steamer schedules. Surprisingly, the former GSN Leith to London passenger steamer *Swift* was bought in late 1929 in order to allow the larger *Aberdonian* to lay up during the slack winter season. Given the name *Harlaw*, she was soon followed by another second-hand passenger-cargo steamer in the form of the Burns & Laird Lines' *Lairdswood*, originally named *Woodcock* in the Burns fleet. This ship had extensive accommodation for 140 First Class passengers as well as comfortable Second Class accommodation, and was given the new name *Lochnagar*.

Further south, the Tyne-Tees Steam Shipping Company operated the *Richard Welford* and *New Londoner* on a twice weekly service between the Tyne and London. Two new quasi-sisters were ordered in 1923, the *Hadrian* from Swan Hunter's yard and the *Bernicia* from Hawthorn Leslie. Both ships had an operational speed of 15 knots to maintain the 24-hour voyage to London. The *Hadrian* could accommodate 170 First Class and 260 Second Class passengers, the *Bernicia* slightly fewer. Both ships carried sixty portable berths in the 'tween decks aft during the tourist season as an extension to the forty Second Class berths available in the poop. In September 1932 the *Hadrian* and *Bernicia* were laid up; both were reactivated in June 1933 for the summer season, after which the London passenger service was withdrawn.

William Sloan & Company commissioned their last passenger cargo steamers in 1924 – the sisters *Brora* and *Beauly* – while losing the elderly *Ettrick* in September when she ran aground in the Bristol Avon. The company also commissioned its last cargo steamer – the *Orchy* – in 1930, and withdrew from passenger-carrying two years later.

Free Trade Wharf in the early 1920s with the Newcastle passenger steamer *Richard Welford* (1908) alongside and the passenger cargo steamer *Dunstanburgh* (1912) anchored off Hubbock's Wharf.

The Tyne-Tees Steam
Shipping Company
steamer *Hadrian*
(1923) coming up
the Thames for her
morning arrival from
Newcastle at the Free
Trade Wharf.

The Clyde Shipping Company, still based at St Katherine Dock, had to rebuild its fleet post-war and persisted with passenger-carriers, recognising a seasonal demand from holiday makers wishing to travel to and from London. A series of variations on a theme were completed for the company in the 1920s, starting with the *Tuskar* and ending with the *Eddystone*. Each ship had excellent First Class accommodation, but only for a modest number of passengers. Meanwhile, no new coastal passenger and cargo liners were commissioned by the newly formed Coast Lines Group in this period.

Malcolm McRonald describes the fate of the Dublin to London service, also based at St Katherine Dock, in his book *The Irish Boats*:

After the [Great] war, B&I's fleet had been reduced by war losses and sales to two ships, *Lady Wimborne* and *Lady Cloë*, with accommodation for 70 passengers each. Two wartime standard ships were bought from the British Government in 1919 after their launch. The *War Spey* was completed as the *Lady Patricia* and the *War Garry* became the *Lady Emerald*. Unlike their predecessors, these two ships had no passenger accommodation. The four ships covered Dublin to London calling at Cork, Falmouth, Torquay and Southampton. There were twice weekly sailings in each direction, one by a passenger ship and one by a cargo ship. The passenger service was reduced in the early 1930s, when most passenger accommodation was removed, leaving only a few cabins for men. All passenger carrying ceased in 1937, but the cargo service continued until 1939.

The City of Cork Steam Packet lost six out of its fleet of eight ships in the First World War. Unable to maintain its peacetime services it was bought by Coast Lines in 1918 and then became part of British & Irish. The passenger service from Cork to London was discontinued.

The sluggish post-war trade forced Coast Lines to reduce its prestigious Liverpool to London passenger and cargo service in 1919 to just one ship. The *Southern Coast* continued her lonely circuit between Liverpool and London calling at intermediate ports as inducement required. She still had substantial passenger accommodation with about eighty berths; popular in the summer months, few of these berths were occupied in the winter and the economics of the service are hard to fathom.

The over-capacity of the *Southern Coast* on the London service was resolved in the early 1930s when two innovative motor ships were commissioned, each with just twelve passenger berths. The new ships were the *British Coast* and *Atlantic Coast*, equipped with engines aft and accommodation and bridge amidships. Built in 1933 and 1934 respectively, they offered 890 tons gross and a service speed of 12 knots derived from a pair of direct reversing oil engines. The obvious success of the motor ships is evident as they were to become the forerunners of a host of engines-aft cargo motor ships in the Coast Lines' fleets, and parents of two more passenger and cargo ships – the *Ocean Coast* and *Pacific Coast* – which were delivered in 1935. These two ten-passenger ships displaced the *British Coast* and *Atlantic Coast* from the Liverpool to London run based at Shadwell Basin.

The Clyde Shipping Company went into the 1930s with its modern fleet of steamers built after the First World War. These ships offered up to sixty First Class and thirty Second Class berths. Typical of the fleet was the war-built *Goodwin* as G. W. Tripp described in an article, which first appeared in *Sea Breezes* October 1955:

> …there were 13 two berth state rooms and 3 four berth, two of which opened out into the dining saloon in which also were two open berths, while round the smoking room on the Boat Deck were five more open berths. Sleeping accommodation was thus provided for 45 passengers, and all was situated amidships. Adjoining the smoking room was the master's cabin.

Round trip fares were available at £4 5s, which could be used for circular tours returning via Edinburgh or Dundee along the east coast – the Glasgow to east coast rail fare being extra. Tripp again:

> For lovers of the sea alone the company arranged for passengers to leave London on the Saturday vessel, reach Glasgow on Tuesday, sail again in the evening for Belfast, the arrival there being next morning, and eventually leave the same day for London, arriving back in the Metropolis on Saturday morning. The fare for this return sea trip was £5.

The peak of design of the west coast coastal passenger and cargo liner was the new sisters *Rathlin* and *Beachy*. These two vessels were the pride of the fleet and maintained the direct Thames to Clyde service calling at Southampton, Plymouth, and Belfast. They could accommodate forty-two First Class passengers, mainly in two-berth cabins, and a further twenty-three Third Class passengers.

No passenger services survived after Second World War, save for the weekly departure from Liverpool to London by Coast Lines twelve-passenger cargo ships. A service was planned from Aberdeen, but this was abandoned as cargo handling disrupted advertised schedules and passenger carrying became untenable. Thus ended the long tradition of sailing from the Pool to UK destinations east and west.

Chapter 8

The European Passenger Liner Trades

A number of British and foreign owned companies operated passenger and cargo liner services from the Pool to the near Continent. Services included various ports in the Baltic, Bremen and Hamburg, Amsterdam and Rotterdam, Ostend and Bordeaux. Passenger carrying fell away during the 1930s and declined rapidly after the Second World War. These services were nevertheless a long-standing and important part of the business of the Pool, including London Dock and St Katherine Dock.

The first liner service from the Pool, based at Brewers Wharf beneath the Tower was that to Calais owned by Messrs W. J. Jolliffe and Sir Edward Banks. It commenced in 1822 with the second ship joining the service the following year. A twice-weekly service was aimed at with the two small wooden-hulled paddle steamers *Lord Melville* and *Earl of Liverpool*; however, maintenance and weather reduced the service at times to occasional departures from either port. At the formation of the General Steam Navigation Company (GSN) in 1924 the steamers became part of the new combine. The Clyde-based steamer *Rapid* was then bought for the Calais service and the *Earl of Liverpool* switched to a new liner service between London and Ostend.

In 1825 a new route to Dunkirk was added and to Rotterdam, the latter importing live cattle into London. All these services carried passengers and some cargo, but they also deviated from schedules to tow sailing ships in and out of the Thames estuary. In 1826 ten ships were deployed on six separate Continental liner services:

To Lisbon, Vigo, Oporto and Gibraltar: *George IV, Duke of York*; irregular departures
To Boulogne: *Rapid*; every Tues and Fri
To Calais: *Attwood, Lord Melville*; every Mon, Wed, Thurs, Sat
To Ostend: *Earl of Liverpool, Mountaineer*; Every Weds, Sat
To Rotterdam: *Belfast*; Every Sat
To Hamburg: *Sir Edward Banks, Hylton Jolliffe*; Every Sat

Passage time varied from 12 hours to Calais to 54 hours to Hamburg and longer still to Gibraltar. The ships were handled at Brewers Wharf/Galley Wharf near the Tower and passengers embarked by tender 'off Custom House or Tower', except for the Gibraltar service, which took passengers aboard off Deptford. In 1828 a new liner service was initiated to Bordeaux; two years later a short-lived service operated by Wigram & Green to Rotterdam was closed in the face of competition from both GSN and NV Nederlandsche Stoomboot Maatschappij. Thus, in a very short space of time, GSN established itself as the leader in the near Continental liner trades, although its shareholders got short shrift as any surplus cash was ploughed straight back into new developments.

GSN consolidated its various Continental services alongside its domestic routes (Chapters 6 and 7). The company commissioned its first iron-hulled paddle steamer in 1837, the *Rainbow*, which it deployed on the Antwerp service. With the development of the St Katherine's Hospital site, GSN was able to secure leasehold on St Katherine's Wharf just downstream of the Tower – this ensured that passengers could board and disembark from the quayside rather than have to summon a boatman to take them out to their ship. However, the French services remained at London Bridge Wharf which had become their home in the 1830s.

By the late 1840s GSN had nearly forty steamers in service. Services from St Katherine's wharf comprised:

To Hamburg: *Caledonia, Countess of Lonsdale, John Bull, Princess Royal, Wilberforce*
To Antwerp: *Giraffe, Ocean, Rainbow*
To Ostend: *Sir Edward Banks, Triton, Venezuela*
To Calais: *Belfast, Earl of Liverpool, Tourist*
To Boulogne: *Harlequin, Star, William Jolliffe*
To Havre: *Columbine, James Watt*

The ships ranged in age from the *Belfast*, which had been built in 1820, to the second iron-hulled steamer, the *Triton*, which was commissioned in 1845. It was not long before the first screw steamer arrived in service, ships such as the *Stork*, completed in 1864 being typical of this new breed of Continental trader. Newbuilding continued as funds allowed and between 1869 and 1872 three new ships were completed for

GSN's Hamburg steamer *Virgo* (1870) in the Lower Pool. [DP World]

the Hamburg service: *Libra, Virgo,* and *Iris.* They had eighty First Class berths aft and seventy-two Second Class in the fo'c'sle. In 1875 the passenger and cargo paddle steamers *Swallow* and *Swift* were commissioned for the daytime service to Ostend; these were the last paddle steamers built for the Continental services, and they remained in service until 1901 when they were in turn replaced by the former railway steamer *Alouette.* She carried hundreds of rabbits from Ostend – a cheap food for the Londoners (ready dressed rabbits retailed at between 6d and a shilling depending on size) and the *Alouette* soon became known as the Ostend Rabbit Boat! She was licensed to carry 325 day passengers in two classes.

Difficult trading conditions in the early 1870s, not least caused by the Franco-German war, forced GSN to close its prestigious Bordeaux service. However, it was reopened in 1876 when new routes to Rotterdam and Harlingen were introduced; all three services were advertised with passenger accommodation. The first purpose-built steel-hulled ships were the *Cygnet* and *Albatross,* which joined the Mediterranean services in 1883 and 1884 offering just twelve berths for passengers. In 1883 the Hamburg service was transferred to Harwich while the French services were also reduced to just twelve passengers. The Hamburg service also served London when the new steamer *Peregrine* was commissioned in 1892.

The *Lapwing* (1879) departing the Upper Pool on a sailing to Hamburg.

The *Peregrine* (1892) was built for the GSN service from London to Hamburg and is seen on the evening departure from the Thames.

In 1890 a fine new steamer was commissioned for the Bordeaux service from St Katherine's Wharf. This was the *Hirondelle*, with accommodation for seventy First Class passengers complete with smoke room and music room, fifty Second Class and twenty-five Third Class passengers, the latter housed in the fo'c'sle. She was fast for her day, managing 15½ knots on trials, and soon became very popular with travellers. The *Hirondelle* and the *Albatross* were displaced from the Bordeaux service by the new passenger cargo steamers *Grive* and *Ortolan* in 1906; this allowed a departure from both ports on Saturdays for the twelve-day return trip. Thus, by the start of the First World War, passengers were carried only on the Bordeaux and Ostend routes in any number and limited berths available on the Dutch and French services and to Oporto.

The *Hirondelle*, which had been serving between Harwich and Hamburg before the war, the *Ortolan,* and the *Grive* were all war losses. The two smaller passenger units in the pre-war Mediterranean service, the *Drake* and *Fauvette*, dating from 1908 and 1912 respectively, were also lost to enemy action. Passenger carrying on the Mediterranean services was reduced to the cargo ships with just twelve passenger berths. Five new ships were delivered after the war for the Mediterranean service, each with engines and accommodation amidships complete with twelve comfortable passenger berths and a small saloon. Thus, between 1920 and 1922, the *Heron, Starling, Halcyon, Philomel,* and *Drake* were commissioned. Of these the *Halcyon* and *Philomel* were the dedicated Bordeaux steamers, but the service was moved from the Thames to Southampton leaving only the daylight service to Ostend as the final passenger liner service operated by the company from the Thames. That being so, a downturn in that trade followed and the *Alouette* closed the Ostend service in 1924.

In 1934 the Southampton terminal for Bordeaux reverted to London but it was an irregular service with only two passenger berths on offer. Happily, in 1936 two new dedicated ships, each equipped for twelve passengers, were commissioned for the Mediterranean services: the steamer *Philomel* and the motor ship *Heron*, delivered in 1936 and 1937 respectively. They had a complicated schedule based on Hays Wharf in the Upper Pool, with departures depending more on cargo handling needs than on regular sailings preferred by passengers. When they returned to civilian duties in 1946, refurbishment left them with only four passenger berths each. Apart from the war years, the pair remained on Mediterranean duties until the mid-1950s when passenger carrying ceased.

The first foreign-owned steam driven liner service out of the Pool was that introduced in 1827 by the Steam Screw Schooner Company of Amsterdam. The 21-metre-long (70 feet) wooden paddle steamer *De Beurs* inaugurated the service between Amsterdam and Fresh Wharf in 1827. Pontoons were needed at Fresh Wharf to keep the vessel upright in deep water. Passengers were carried from the outset and inbound cargoes included dairy produce and other foods, while exports mainly comprised manufactured goods. In 1855 the Amsterdam Steamship Company was incorporated to take over the service, which by now had migrated to Brewers Wharf on the north bank adjacent to the Tower.

A key competitor was the Batavia Line, running between the Pool and Rotterdam. Lord Ambrose Greenway describes the early days of the company in his book *A Century of North Sea Passenger Steamers*:

On 12 April 1830, following unsuccessful attempts to start a Rotterdam-Hamburg service and later one between Antwerp and London, NV Nederlandsche Stoomboot Maats. inaugurated a Rotterdam-London link with the 300 ton wooden paddle steamer *De Batavia* (1829). The service prospered and over the years two more paddlers and four screw-driven steamers were added, all built of iron in the company's own shipyard, the last being the 760 ton *Fijenoord* of 1879.

In 1895 NSM decided to concentrate entirely on shipbuilding and accordingly sold the London service with its ships and goodwill to Messrs Wm. H Muller & Co., with the proviso that it should continue under the Batavia Line banner. Mullers formed a new company, the Netherlands Cargo & Passenger Steamship Co. and quickly ordered two new steel ships from Gourlay Brothers of Dundee, enabling a daily service (excluding Sundays) to be started to Custom House Quay.

In 1879 the Holland Steamship Company (Hollandsche Stoomboot Maatschappij) took over the Steam Screw Schooner Company of Amsterdam. The Holland Steamship Company introduced the 'stroom' nomenclature for its ships, renaming the *Fijenoord*, which it acquired from the Netherlands Steamship Company, the *Ijstroom*. A second ship, the *Amstelstroom*, became her running mate in 1885 allowing, for the first time, a twice-weekly service between the two ports. The *Amstelstroom* offered accommodation for passengers in two classes and her compound engine allowed the passage between ports to be made in little over 16 hours.

Two ships joined the HSM service in 1898 and 1900 – the new sisters *Ijstroom* and *Maastroom*. These ships offered First and Second Class berths and in addition provided facilities for steerage passengers. They had an unusual four island profile but each could be identified by the thickness of the funnel; one having been completed in Sunderland the other two years later in Rotterdam. The pair established a rigid schedule with departures from Brewers Wharf at 8 a.m. on Wednesdays and Saturdays and at 4 p.m. the same day from Amsterdam. The *Ijstroom* was swept against London Bridge in windy conditions on a rising tide in 1912, losing her mainmast and causing damage to various items in the after part of the ship.

A new *Amstelstroom* joined the service in 1910 – the first ship to offer refrigerated chambers for the carriage of perishable dairy products, including butter, cheese, poultry, and eggs. She was used both on the London service and that to Hull. However, her tenure was short-lived as she was lost in the North Sea during the First World War; the basic services continued throughout the war, although at a depleted schedule due to slower turnaround times at the ports and military restrictions over passage routes and sailing times. In January 1918 the *Maastroom* was damaged in the Pool during a German air raid, but was repaired and after the war refurbished with just twelve passenger berths. Her sister, the *Ijstroom,* was sold, being replaced by the *Lingestroom* – a product of the Rotterdam Drydock Company and completed in 1917.

A near sister, the *Zaanstroom,* had been captured by the Germans and later scuttled at Zeebrugge. She was eventually raised and later saw regular service from the Pool when she was acquired by the United Baltic Corporation and renamed *Baltannic*.

The *Zaanstroom* initially offered just twelve passengers, but additional berths were added, bringing the total to twenty-five. The ships were berthed from then at Fennings Wharf. Goods were transhipped by canal, road, and rail throughout Europe via Amsterdam; distribution in Britain was accomplished by sending ships also to a number of regional ports including Manchester, Hull, Leith, and Bristol. By the later 1930s passenger carrying became less important, although some berths were still available on the London service. During the Second World War all services ceased and the ships were available to the British and one, the *Hontestroom*, was converted for use as a Convoy Rescue Ship, although was found inadequate in this role after attachment to only six Atlantic convoys.

In 1946 the Dutch service moved to enlarged and more modern facilities at Chambers Wharf below Tower Bridge. This gave better road access and provided modern refrigerated storage space. Passengers were no longer carried and dedicated and modern refrigerated cargo ships were allocated to the route. Arrivals at London were scheduled for cargo handling to start at 6 p.m. to enable goods to be in the market the following morning. The record number of eggs unloaded from one ship amounted to just under 3 million!

One of the last ships built for the London service was the *Texelstroom*, although she also served on other routes as required. The *Texelstroom* was completed in 1962 at Arnhem and offered every modern facility. She had an array of electrically driven deck cranes and all the hatches had reinforced tank tops to enable the use of forklift trucks in the holds. The deck hatches were electrically driven and could be opened in just one minute. She was faster than the old steamships being capable of a service speed of 14 knots and had a bow thrust unit to facilitate berthing. Sadly, the service was overtaken by the onset of roll-on roll-off traffic from Tilbury and later also between Harwich and the Hook of Holland, and it closed from the Pool in 1974.

The London base of the rival Batavia Line remained in the Upper Pool at Custom House Wharf on the north bank of the river. The ships called at Gravesend for passengers from 1922, via the direct rail link into central London. The key passenger ships had Batavia names; *Batavia II* and *Batavia III*, dating from 1897, were the first ships built for Wm. Muller and could accommodate forty-four First Class, twenty-seven Second Class, and up to 250 steerage passengers on the newly upgraded daily service. They were followed by a larger pair in 1903, *Batavia IV* and *Batavia V,* which had seventy-five First Class berths and twenty-eight Second Class, with space provided for 325 in steerage. A relief ship, *Batavia VI,* was also completed at the same time but she only had limited passenger accommodation. *Batavia II* and *Batavia V* were war losses and were replaced in 1921 by ships with the same names.

The plain yellow and black topped funnel colours of the original Netherlands Steamship Company were changed to Muller Line colours in 1903. The attractive red, white and black colours adorned with a white 'M' are seen in many contemporary images of the Upper Pool as the ships lay alongside Custom House Wharf. The Batavia

The *Batavia IV* (1903) at Custom House Quay seen beneath the stern of the *Baltabor* (1911) on the other side of the Upper Pool.

The *Batavia II* (1921) alongside Custom House Quay in the early 1950s, with Billingsgate and Fresh Wharf beyond the Custom House.

Line route was extremely popular with passengers who enjoyed comfortably furnished accommodation and a reliable daily service between the two ports. The company was only able to return to its berth in the Upper Pool in 1947, once bomb-damaged quayside warehouses had been rebuilt; in the meantime, the immediate post-war service was operated from Harwich. The service to London only closed in 1958 when the *Batavia V* was finally withdrawn and sold for scrap.

The German-owned company Norddeutscher Lloyd entered the London trade from Germany in October 1857 when the purpose-built steamer *Adler* first arrived in St Katherine Dock. She was joined by five more passenger and cargo ships: *Mowe, Falke, Schwalbe, Condor,* and *Schwan*. Between them they maintained an approximately-weekly service to London from either Bremen or Hamburg, serving also Hull and Leith. Five new iron-hulled ships were built for the UK service between 1870 and 1884, followed by two steel-hulled ships – the *Albatross* and *Falke*. These ships could accommodate twenty-five First Class passengers and thirty-five in Second Class, the latter berthed in the 'tween decks. They were also equipped to carry cattle in the 'tween decks. These facilities were specially ventilated for the purpose. The last of the iron-hulled ships, the *Adler*, was unique in the fleet as she had two imposing funnels.

From 1885 Norddeutscher Lloyd embarked on a programme of shipbuilding for both its prestigious New York passenger service and for a new commitment to the Far East. In order to do this it determined to sell the ships and goodwill in its UK interests. Thus, in 1897, the UK part of its trade was sold to the Argo Line of Bremen, along with seven steamers. The new owners set about rebuilding the fleet with modern and well-equipped ships that could carry between ten and twenty First Class passengers, twenty-four Second Class, and up to eighty-four in so-called Third Class – the latter comprising unberthed accommodation. The new ships were called *Shwalbe, Sperber, Strauss,* and *Adler* and they were completed between 1898 and 1900.

The company continued to order new ships up until the First World War and a further six ships were delivered by 1913. The *Möwe* was one of the last ships to be completed before the war and she was commissioned as the dedicated London steamer, but she had no provision for cattle. She was a standard three-island type ship with two decks and accommodation for up to forty passengers. The *Möwe* maintained a weekly departure from St Katherine Dock, but did not return to the London route after the war and was in any case sold in 1926. From 1936 onwards the London to Hamburg cargo service was pooled with GSN, allowing a daily departure.

The Argo Line did not build any new passenger ships until 1936 when the *Fasan* was delivered for the route to Hull. The *Schwan* and *Reiher* were completed at Kiel in 1938 for the Bremen to London and Leith to Bremen services. All three ships were badly damaged in the Second World War. Only the *Fasan* was rebuilt for use by the Argo Line, but she was not deployed on the London service.

In 1950 the London trade received three new ships each with accommodation for up to sixty passengers. These were the motor ships *Adler* and *Falke* and another steamship named *Möwe*, but the London passenger service was not reinstated until 1952, and then only on an irregular basis and ceasing altogether shortly afterwards. The company then focussed on its own Baltic passenger trade from Bremen and its passenger and cargo service between Bremen and Hull. London was served by cargo-only vessels, of modern design best suited to the trade, but these ceased to operate when the company focussed entirely on Hull in the 1960s, with a service to Bremen operated by two roll-on roll-off commercial vehicle carriers.

A late entry into the passenger liner trade, based at the Hays Wharf complex on the south bank of the Upper Pool, was the United Baltic Corporation. Philip Kershaw wrote in *Sea Breezes*, February 1961:

> At the end of the First World War, passenger and cargo services between Britain and the Baltic States were so disorganised that many potentially important shipping centres in Latvia, Lithuania and Estonia had no direct links with the Thames. To meet this situation the United Baltic Corporation Ltd. was formed by agreement between Andrew Weir & Co. Ltd., of London, owners of the Bank Line, and the East Asiatic Company of Copenhagen, whose subsidiary, the Russian East Asiatic Company of St Petersburg, had been active in the Baltic since 1899.

The Corporation was registered in May 1919 with a capital of £2 million. Short-term charters were arranged with the East Asiatic Company for their steamers *St Croix*, *St Thomas*, *Reval,* and *Libau*. Within a few months the first pair were bought outright and renamed *Baltriger* and *Baltannic* respectively and the *Libau* as well, which became the *Baltabor*. The first two ships offered twenty-four First and twenty-four Second Class berths, and were also licensed to carry eighty-five Tourist Class passengers. The three ships were advertised to sail to Danzig and Libau and shortly afterwards also to Riga and Reval (Tallinn) from a berth in the East India Docks. However, by 1922 the company realised that they needed refrigerated cargo handling space and moved its London base to Hays Wharf in the Upper Pool. All sailings used the Keil Canal.

By 1924 sailings had settled down to a routine. Departures for Reval and Riga were on Thursdays and to Danzig, Memel and Libau on Friday – except when winter ice conditions interrupted the pattern. Gdynia was added to the sailing lists in 1930, but otherwise there was little change. Several alterations to the fleet, however, took place. The *Baltabor* was sold in 1925 being replaced by the former Royal Mail Line Caribbean feeder ship *Berbice*, which joined the UBC fleet in 1925 as the *Baltara*. This acquisition allowed a full complement of passengers to be carried on each sailing. The original *Baltannic* was now found lacking and was replaced by a new *Baltannic*, which was purchased from Dutch owners in July 1925. She was none other than the one time *Zaanstroom*, built in 1913 for the Hollandsche Stoomboot Maartschappij. During the First World War she had been captured by a German submarine and taken to Zeebrugge where she was scuttled; raised by a team from the Royal Navy, the hulk was condemned and bought by a Dutch firm, refurbished, and renamed *Westland*. Refurbished once again she took up service from Hays Wharf to Tallinn, offering comfortable passenger accommodation with attractive public rooms.

Expansion and upgrading of services saw two acquisitions in 1926, in March the *Baltrader* took up service from the Pool and in December she was followed by the *Baltonia*. The *Baltrader* came from the East Asiatic Company and the *Baltonia* from the British & African Steam Navigation Company (Elder Dempster). The latter ship had accommodation for 150 passengers in two classes and was placed on the weekly service from the Pool to Gdynia. The *Baltara* was wrecked in January 1929 when she grounded in rough weather on passage from Libau to Gdynia; all forty-three passengers and forty crew were landed safely. The *Baltabor* was lost in similar circumstances later in the year when she grounded on an island off the Estonian coast on 26 December. Her crew and two passengers were also safely landed.

Upgrading of the passenger service continued in 1930 when the twenty-nine-year-old Swedish Lloyd passenger liner *Patricia* was acquired, and one-time member of the Russian East Asiatic Company. She had been employed on the Tilbury to Gothenburg service after the war but was displaced by newly built steamers on that route in 1929. UBC paid £32,000 for the ship and renamed her *Baltavia*. She offered excellent passenger accommodation and was extremely popular with travellers.

The GSN steamer *Starling*, built in 1920 for its Mediterranean services, was acquired in January 1930 and renamed *Baltallinn* to run between the Pool and Tallinn, offering twelve passenger berths. So pleased was the Corporation with this purchase that they also took her sister the *Heron* when she came on the market a few years later in 1935; she was renamed *Balteako*. In the meantime, two First World War standard cargo ships of the C Type were bought to assist with cargo shipments; both were equipped with substantial refrigerated compartments for the carriage of perishable foodstuffs, including eggs. Another important acquisition in 1935 was the Furness Withy liner *Dominica*, formerly Johnston Warren lines *Digby*, built in 1913, for the Liverpool to

The *Baltraffic* (1918), one of two standard wartime ships bought by the United Baltic Corporation in 1933, departing from the Upper Pool.

St John's and Halifax passenger service. She was latterly the *Dominica* on the West Indian service, operated from Canada and New York. Renamed *Baltrover*, she became a popular ship with passenger on the service from Hays Wharf to Gdynia and Danzig. She offered sixty-four cabin passenger berths and 130 Third Class; essentially her public rooms were unchanged since her Caribbean days. In the Second World War the Ministry of War Transport put her back on her old transatlantic routes; she did not revert to the UBC after the war.

Two more passenger ships were acquired in 1937 when the *Chimu* and *Cumbal* were bought from the Panama Mail Steamship Company, which was owned by the Grace Line of New York. They were built in Sweden in 1924 and designed for the service from San Francisco to Panama and thence to ports in Central America. They had comfortable accommodation for sixty First Class and sixty Tourist Class passengers, which was always popular with round trip 'cruise' passengers. However, on joining the UBC fleet both ships had the accommodation rebuilt with just twelve passenger berths on offer – the *Chimu* becoming the *Baltavia* and the *Cumbal* the *Baltbor*. Two small Norwegian steamers with limited passenger accommodation were also acquired in 1936 and 1937, being renamed *Baltonia* and *Baltanglia* and intended for the Lithuanian routes. The company was restructured in the late 1930s with the main units deployed as described by Philip Kershaw:

> …three subsidiary companies were registered to operate the Corporation's Baltic traders . These were the Anglo-Latvian Steamship Co. Ltd. (*Baltabor* and *Balteako*), the Anglo-Lithuanian Steamship Co. Ltd. (*Baltanglia* and *Baltonia*) and the Anglo-Estonian Co. Ltd. (*Baltavia* and *Baltallinn*). Each of these companies had its own houseflag, a slightly modified version of the UBC 'foul anchor' on grounds of varying colour, similar to the East Asiatic houseflag, which also includes a 'foul anchor'.

At the end of Second World War the Corporation was left with just six ships: *Baltannic, Baltara, Baltavia, Baltraffic, Baltrover,* and *Balteako,* and urgently sought to redevelop its fleet. However, passenger-carrying in any significant numbers was now a thing of the past. New acquisitions post-war included the *Baltrover*, completed in 1949 for Norwegian owners. She was used on the run to Gdynia by the UBC with just four passenger berths from 1950 onwards. A series of very smart motor ships was commissioned from 1953 onwards with accommodation offered for just two passengers in 'the owners cabin'. The first of this class was the *Baltic Express,* which was accepted from the builders in Germany in March 1953. She was the first purpose built ship that UBC had ever ordered – all other acquisitions being from the second-hand market.

Thus, like other companies before them, the UBC was eventually reduced to a cargo-only liner service, carrying passengers only on an occasional basis. In the early 1970s the unit load services from the Pool were closed in favour of roll-on roll-off traffic focussed at other UK ports. Purfleet became the Thames terminal and then Felixstowe when even larger vessels such as the *Baltic Eider* were commissioned in the late 1980s.

GSN's cargo ship *Albatross* (1943) alongside in the Upper Pool with the United Baltic Corporation steamer *Baltavia* (1924) preparing to depart. [DP World]

The *Baltic Sun* (1962) alongside Tower Bridge Wharf was one of the last conventional cargo ships built for the United Baltic Corporation. [Author]

Ultimate demise of the trade from the Pool was caused by the move towards big container and roll-on roll-off vehicle carriers such as United Baltic Corporation's *Baltic Eider* (1989), working from Felixstowe. [Author]

A partner company to the UBC was that of MacAndrews & Company. It was founded in the 1850s as Robert MacAndrew & Company of London, later also of Seville and Barcelona, in order to satisfy Spanish legal requirements. The first arrival in the Pool was the *Acor*, which came in from Cadiz in March 1859. By the 1870s, a fortnightly sailing was offered from both London, Millwall Dock, and Liverpool to a variety of Spanish ports. Inbound, the steamers docked at Fresh Wharf below London Bridge to unload fruit – mainly oranges – imported from Spain. In the *Weekly Shipping List*, 4 September 1880, the *Pinzon* was loading at London for Barcelona, the *Bilbao* for Bilbao, and the *Zurbaran* for Seville, Cadiz, and other Spanish ports. Passengers were only catered for by special arrangement at this stage.

Hard times befell the company after the First World War and it was taken over in 1917 by the Sir Owen Philipps' Royal Mail group. Passenger-carrying was introduced on a more formal basis in 1921 with the introduction of the first motor ships in the fleet, the *Pizarro* and *Pinzon*, which advertised six berths on their routine sailings from the Pool. In 1924 a new express service was introduced by the steamer *Cortes* for Barcelona. Five more P Class motor ships were added to the fleet in the late 1930s, each continuing with the Spanish celebrity nomenclature. The ships were modified in the early 1930s to accommodate six passengers in three twin-berth cabins. In 1935 the Royal Mail group was obliged to sell MacAndrews & Company to what later became a subsidiary of the Andrew Weir Group, the same founder interests of the United Baltic

Corporation. In 1937 the motor ships *Pozarica* and *Palomares* joined the fleet each with twelve passenger berths. Philip Kershaw wrote in *Sea Breezes*, May 1965:

> Cruises by the motor ships were advertised for as little as £16 for a 16 to 17 days trip to the Canaries and on some routes 25 day round voyages cost £1 a day. The steamers also carried occasional [liner] passengers and rates were quoted on request, according to advertisements of the period.

Between the wars the Curry Line of Leith also joined the London to Mediterranean Conference. It bought the goodwill of a London-based company formerly trading in this area, although it did not acquire any of its ships. Some of the Curry Line vessels offered a small number of passenger berths and round trips could be obtained by arrangement with the London agent.

MacAndrews resumed services after the Second World War with fortnightly departures from London Dock to Spanish ports, returning to discharge at Butler's Wharf. Another service called at Casablanca, Tangier, and Ceuta, also loading at London Dock with departures on alternate Fridays, and there was also a Gibraltar and Barcelona service. Most ships offered at least four berths for passengers, including the post-war built *Pinto* and *Pelayo*. In the early 1950s ships were built to the same design as UBC's *Baltic Exporter*: the *Velazquez*, *Valdes*, and *Villegas*, commissioned in 1954 and 1954, each

MacAndrews & Company's cargo ship *Villegas* (1955) alongside in London Dock in the late 1950s, with large boxed machinery being loaded onto a lighter for onward shipment overseas.

MacAndrews' *Palomares* (1963) unloading Spanish fruit at Fresh Wharf in the late 1960s.

with twelve passenger berths. Subsequent ships did not carry passengers and yet again the break bulk trade was finally overtaken by containerisation in the early 1970s.

Nowadays it is hard to imagine the buoyant international passenger trade that was carried out from the Pool, Upper and Lower. Much of this was not renewed after the Second World War when it became more convenient to travel to near European destinations by train, crossing the Channel to Boulogne for the onward rail connection. The Baltic connection was still made by sea but via existing regular passenger services, such as Swedish Lloyd service to Gothenburg and the various ferry connections to Danish and German ports. In due course these were overtaken by the airplane and nowadays by cheap no-frills airline operators willing to take you to the Mediterranean or the Baltic at little more than cost.

The cargo trade was always more important in economic terms than the passenger trade. Britain exported manufactured goods in return for agricultural produce in an essential exchange that kept its factories in full employment and fed its workers, and the Pool of London remained central to this trade throughout the 1960s, only losing it to the roll-on roll-off vehicle ferry and the container ship in the 1970s. The wharves of the Pool were instrumental in developing this trade from the very early days of the steamship and even before that when sailing ships from the Netherlands and Belgium arrived with grain and other goods, while schooners from southern France tied up at Fresh Wharf laden with huge barrels of wine. Throughout the steamship era and into that of the motor ship, companies such as GSN maintained a fleet of cargo ships supporting the Continental and Mediterranean services – these companies and their ships are far too great in number and variety to describe in this volume, although their important role must not be overlooked.

Chapter 9

Royal and Other Visitors

For over 1,000 years, monarchs and royalty have made their homes along the Thames in London: at Greenwich, Rotherhithe, the Tower, Bridewell, Whitehall, and Westminster. Since Tudor times, the Thames has provided a celebratory route for royal events and processions, including arrivals, departures, receptions, coronations, weddings, and christenings. King Henry VIII owned two royal barges, the *Lyon* and *Greyhound*, which served his riverside palaces, and were kept at the Royal Bargehouse at Lambeth. Later monarchs commissioned smaller barges and shallops for ceremonial and pleasure use on the Thames.

Royal barges and shallops were soon imitated by the Lord Mayor and the City Livery Companies. In all, sixty-eight Livery companies came to own, or hire, barges for ceremonial occasions on the Thames. As well as having a presence at many royal-related river events, the Livery Companies' barges also attended the incoming Lord Mayor's annual waterborne procession to Westminster. Until 1856, when the Lord Mayor's Thames processions ceased, royal and other river events were hugely popular and well attended; these events were usually watched by thousands of spectators, many of whom took to the water in wherries – the traditional sharp-ended rowing boats of the Thames watermen.

The Tower and the Tower Dock were regularly used by royalty arriving and departing from other palaces along the river. Famously, Anne Boleyn – second wife of the young King Henry VIII – disembarked at Tower Dock twice; the first time for her coronation as Queen of England, a lavish ceremony held in the Tower of London on 1 June 1533, and the second time on 2 May 1536 for her trial under charges that she was a witch, that she was promiscuous, and that she had held an incestuous relationship with her brother George. Evidence for these charges had been trumped up out of thin air and the Queen was beheaded by sword at the order of the King. Her five alleged suitors were similarly dealt with. Anne's surviving daughter with Henry VIII later, of course, became Queen Elizabeth I.

Much of the traditional pageant, however, took place above the Pool, as, for example, Jonathan Schneer recounts in his book *The Thames: England's River*:

> In 1660 the Stuart family regained the throne. Almost immediately Charles II, son of Charles I, sought to make use of the river as his ancestors had done. He planned to travel by royal barge down the Thames, from Hampton Court to Whitehall with his bride, Catherine of Braganza, on 23 August 1662. On 29 July someone from the Court contacted the Lord Mayor of London, who in turn issued instructions to the twelve great livery companies of the City: the king 'expects such demonstration of affection from this Cittie as hath bin vsual upon so great & solemne occasione'. It seems obvious that Charles wanted more than merely to please and impress Catherine of Braganza...
>
> The people of London certainly played their part in this drama. In fact, on the appointed day the City outdid itself on Charles's behalf. According to the great seventeenth century diarist John Evelyn, 'Aqua Triumphalis', as the extravaganza was termed, 'had been the most magnificent triumph ever floted on the Thames, considering the innumerable number of boates & Vessels, dressd and adornd with all imaginable Pomp: but above all, the Thrones, Arches, Pageants & other representations, stately barges of the Lord Mayor & Companies, with various Inventions, musique, & Peales of Ordnance both from the vessels and shore'. Ten thousand boats (in Samuel Pepys's estimation) came out that day, so that the river all but disappeared from view, except for a narrow channel in the middle left open for the King whose own barge grandest of all was hung with crimson damask and bore a canopy of cloth of gold supported by Corinthian pillars themselves weathered with ribbons and garlands of flowers.

In the nineteenth century Queen Victoria tended to favour Greenwich rather than the Pool as an embarkation point for her travels. This almost certainly reflected the stench coming off the river nearer the city, at least in the early part of her reign. Any ceremonies in the city tended to be surrounded by numerous bouquets of sweet smelling flowers, although these did little to disguise the scent of the sewage flowing down-river. The Queen's ancient royal yacht *Royal George* was last used to convey the new Monarch to Leith in 1842. The history of GSNC (Robins) reports:

> The reign of Victoria had an auspicious start when the young Queen opted to travel aboard one of GSN's newest fleet members, the paddle steamer *Trident*, rather than her own royal yacht. GSN offered to make the steamer available to the Monarch for her visit to Scotland in September 1842, the *Trident* being a superior vessel to the royal sailing yacht HMY *Royal George*, which was manned by a scratch crew from the Reserve whenever it was in service. Although the Queen and Prince Albert sailed north on the royal yacht, they opted to return courtesy of GSN. The royal party was delighted with the accommodation provided and enjoyed a fast 48 hour passage back to the Thames. It appears that the *Trident*, in company with the GSN steamer *Monarch*, which conveyed the royal baggage, set off from the Forth at the same time as the royal yacht and other official vessels. By dusk on the first day, only the two

GSN vessels were in convoy, the Government ships having been left far astern. Within a year, of course, by Royal insistence, the new HMY *Victoria and Albert* had been designed, built at Pembroke Dockyard and delivered in time for an inaugural summer coastal cruise.

The *Trident* disembarked her Royal passengers at Woolwich before proceeding up the smelly river to return to normal duties. GSNC was not slow to point out that it was, of course, now 'by Royal Appointment'.

The new paddle steamer HMY *Victoria and Albert* rarely visited the Pool. She was slow and her royal apartments were at best uncomfortable, and described at the time as 'very ordinary'. She was replaced in 1855 by a new Royal Yacht, also named *Victoria and Albert,* and this ship tended to embark and disembark members of the royal family at Gravesend, using the train to connect to London or at Portsmouth. The Pool was considered too much of a busy commercial centre for the royal yacht to enter, and even the third HMY *Victoria and Albert*, commissioned in 1901 – too late for Queen Victoria to use – very rarely came up to the Pool.

By way of contrast, Her Majesty Queen Elizabeth II has numerous ceremonial memories of the Pool, including arrivals and departures in the last of the royal yachts, the *Britannia*. The earliest ceremonial occasion on the river that Queen Elizabeth II took part in was the Royal River Pageant, held on 22 July 1953, six weeks after the coronation and organised by the Lord Mayor. The Queen attended in the Port of London Authority's inspection launch, *Nore*, which functioned as the Royal Barge. The Queen's Silver Jubilee was celebrated by a River Progress and Pageant, held on the 9 June 1977, wherein over 140 vessels took part. The Queen embarked in the second of the PLA's launches to be called *Nore*; again the vessel was dressed for the occasion as the royal barge. The Queen's Golden Jubilee, in 2002, was also marked by a tribute event, timed to coincide with the regular Thames Festival. Her Majesty the Queen last came to the Pool to lead her Thames Diamond Jubilee Procession on Sunday 3 June 2012. This comprised a large flotilla of vessels, but the weather was appalling with low cloud and persistent rain, although this did not deter from the magnificence of the occasion.

The Queen and royal family have often embarked in the royal yacht *Britannia* when in the Pool. The maiden voyage of the yacht ended on the 15 May 1954, when the Queen and royal family returned in HMY *Britannia* to London, following a six-month tour of the Commonwealth. The ship came into the Pool and moored at Battle Bridge Tier below London Bridge, buoys often used by visiting warships. The buoys had to be reset for the *Britannia* and were separated by an additional 36 m (110 feet) to 149 m (490 feet) separation. The Queen and her new royal yacht received a rapturous welcome from thousands of onlookers, including the port workers, lining the riverbank and looking down from both Tower Bridge and London Bridge. The new royal yacht had sailed to Fiji to meet the Shaw Savill Line's *Gothic,* which had acted as the royal yacht for all but the last leg of the tour.

The *Britannia* returned to the Pool many times. For example, in August 1990, Her Majesty Queen Elizabeth the Queen Mother embarked on HMY *Britannia* in the Pool

A commemorative plate by Royal Doulton: 'Queen of the Seas', the royal yacht *Britannia* arriving in the Upper Pool, by Roy Huxley.

of London to celebrate her ninetieth birthday. In 1994, the Prince of Wales joined the royal yacht on the river for an event to mark the centenary anniversary of Tower Bridge. Symbolically, when *Britannia* made her final visit to London, in November 1997, the Queen, the Duke of Edinburgh, and the Prince of Wales held a special farewell lunch, moored opposite HMS *Belfast*.

The royal yacht was also used by other members of the royal family. One homecoming to the Pool was especially memorable; HRH Princess Margaret and her new husband Antony Armstrong-Jones arrived in the Pool on 4 May 1980 from their honeymoon in the Caribbean.

Among the foreign royal yachts that have visited the Pool, the Danish royal family's yacht *Dannebrog* is perhaps the best known. She last came up to the Upper Pool in August 2012 during the London Olympics, looking like a traditional yacht with bowsprit and gilded crowns at bow and stern. The yacht was built in 1931 and has a crew of fifty-seven while Queen Margrethe and the Prince are on board.

The 'Q' ship *Suffolk Coast* (1917) lying alongside a German U-boat U-155 in St Katherine Dock, London at the start of her tour as a show boat.

Military visits to the Pool have always attracted a great deal of attention. One of these was the arrival of the Q Ship HMS *Southern Coast* in St Katherine Dock during a round-Britain tour at the end of the First World War. The *Suffolk Coast* was requisitioned in August 1918 and converted into the heavily armed and disguised 'Q' ship HMS *Suffolk Coast*. She received a 4-inch gun mounted on a hydraulic lift in No. 1 hatch, which could be brought rapidly to upper deck level once a U-boat was lulled within range. Part of the sham was a panic crew that would rush to the lifeboats and prepare the boats for launching, so distracting attention from the ship's gun crews while they took up their stations. Canvas deck houses, ventilators and funnels were available, coupled with a variety of names painted on the bow and different ensigns at the stern. However, the White Ensign had to be shown immediately prior to engagement. While many of the Q ships were lost, the *Suffolk Coast* was commissioned too late to be of service. Harold Auten in his book on Q ships tells the story of the *Suffolk Coast*; she was requisitioned at his suggestion:

On November 10th we sailed from Queenstown to test her guns. Owing to bad weather she had to put into Milford Haven on the following day, only to be greeted by the hoarse-throated hooters of all the ships in the neighbourhood – it was the Armistice.... On the day following we left for Plymouth... Out of Plymouth we proceeded to test our guns, which seemed rather farcical under the circumstances, but it had to be done. Then we were told that we were to become a show ship and tour round the ports of England, telling people how it had been done.

The other unusual visitor to St Katherine Dock was the U-boat *U-155*, which surrendered on 24 November 1918 and was brought to London to be exhibited alongside the *Southern Coast*. The U-boat was commissioned as the merchant submarine *Deutschland* – a blockade-breaking German merchant submarine used during the First World War. She was developed with private funds and operated by the North German Lloyd Line. After making two voyages as an unarmed merchantman, she was taken over by the German Imperial Navy on 19 February 1917 and converted into *U-155*, armed with six torpedo tubes and two deck guns. *U-155* sank forty-three Allied ships during her military career, an aggregate of 120,434 tons gross.

The many military visitors to the Upper Pool over the years creates a long list of ships ranging from small minesweepers and motor torpedo boats up to HMS *Belfast* herself. For example, the state-of-the-art submarines HMS *Swordfish* and HMS *Starfish* were open to the public in the Upper Pool in May 1937 as a demonstration of Britain's naval capability in a Europe that was becoming less and less politically stable. A similar visit was made in 1939 when the submarines HMS *Otway* and HMS *Osiris* were berthed in Shadwell Basin. In 1951 Shadwell Basin again hosted the visit of two submarines, HMS *Auriga* and HMS *Acheron* – this time to celebrate the fiftieth

U-155 having surrendered on 24 November 1918 was brought to London and put on exhibition. She was built with commercial money and was originally named *Deutschland*.

anniversary of the Submarine Service. The Bay Class frigate HMS *Mounts Bay* lay off Custom House Quay on a promotional visit for a short while in 1955; she had just been refitted ready for service in the West Indies. The newly commissioned Tribal Class frigate HMS *Ashanti* was in the Pool in 1962 – and so the list goes on.

There was the occasional incident to the visitors in the Pool. The Leander Class frigate HMS *Jupiter* spent a week at Battle Bridge Tier in June 1984. At the end of her stay she was pulled away from the buoys, but completely misjudging the current, fell broadside across the central pier of London Bridge, while forty seamen standing to attention on the after deck had to run for safety. Additional tugs were brought to help and twenty minutes later HMS *Jupiter* was freed from her perch to the accompaniment of enthusiastic applause from an exited gathering of sightseers watching on the bridge. The ship, with a badly dented hull, hastily withdrew from the Pool while engineers checked the structural integrity of the bridge before road traffic was allowed to resume.

Foreign naval visitors included a pair of Danish frigates shown off in the Upper Pool during February 1958, which lay off New Fresh Wharf. A number of NATO warships came into the Pool in 1959 helping to celebrate the Queen's thirty-third birthday, but again, the list of such visitors is extensive.

The Pool of London has become an important venue for showing off new ships and advertising their trade. One of the first departures from the traditional naming of a ship by its sponsor at its launch was the naming ceremony held aboard the new banana carrier *Geestbay* in July 1964. She came from her builders in Amsterdam up the Thames and through Tower Bridge to berth bows upstream at New Fresh Wharf – she was a big ship for the Pool, being some 7,891 tons gross. The new ship made quite an impact with passers-by on London Bridge with an all-white hull and superstructure topped by modernistic twin-exhaust uptakes. Dressed overall while in the Pool, her naming ceremony over, and the last of the visitors ashore, she headed down-river to take up her commercial duties between Barry in South Wales and Eastern Caribbean ports. She offered comfortable First Class accommodation for twelve passengers and had chilled space for a typical load of 12 million bananas.

New ferries have also been shown off in the Upper Pool to attract custom to their services. The French cross-Channel ferry *Cote d'Azur* is one example, the West Highland ferry *Clansman* is another – the latter with an exhibition on tourism in Scotland and Scottish interests. In June 1967 the vehicle ferry *Dragon* came alongside New Fresh Wharf to champion the new service between Southampton and Le Havre to be operated by Normandy Ferries. After spending a couple of days in London open to the travel trade and for inspection by London-based staff of parent company GSN, she carried out berthing trials at Southampton and Le Havre before being opened to the public at Southampton. She commenced service on 29 June 1967.

In recent year HMS *Belfast* has become a popular berth for showing off new ships and naming ceremonies. One of the first of these naming ceremonies was conducted by the Lady Mayoress of London in October 1976 when the Dutch ocean-going salvage tug *Smit London* arrived for her official naming ceremony on 8 October. The *Smit London* was built largely with the offshore oil industry in mind and was owned by Smit International Ocean Towage and Salvage Company. While she was in the Pool,

The new Hebridean ferry *Clansman* (1964) on a visit to the Pool to promote Sottish interests and tourism. [Donald Meek collection]

The new vehicle ferry *Dragon* (1967) belonging to Normandy Ferries, lying alongside New Fresh Wharf in June 1967 for inspection by the travel trade and GSN staff at London.

The Trinity House coastal support vessel *Galatea* arriving in the Pool of London prior to her naming by Her Majesty Queen Elizabeth II on 17 October 2007.

the opportunity was taken to show her off to the London-based insurance companies – some of which quite possibly could require her services at some time in the future.

Another significant christening alongside HMS *Belfast* was that of the Trinity House coastal support vessel *Galatea*. On Wednesday 17 October 2007, Her Majesty Queen Elizabeth II boarded the vessel to be greeted by the Duke of Edinburgh in his capacity as Master of Trinity House. After a tour of the new vessel the Queen was asked to press a button to release the traditional bottle of champagne which then smashed against the ship's hull. Among the array of high-tech devices aboard the ship is a 'moon pool' that allows access through the bottom of the ship.

One of the largest vessels to be christened alongside HMS *Belfast* was the new 16,000 tons gross vehicle ferry *Adeline*. Owned by CLdN of Luxembourg, she was christened in a ceremony held on Friday 26 October 2012. Ms Alice Walpole, British Ambassador to Luxembourg, accepted the role of godmother to the new ship and concluded the ceremony with the traditional breaking of a bottle of champagne against the hull of the ship.

Not only do new ships come up to the Pool to show off, some old ships also come to say goodbye. The RMS *St Helena*, that had served that island since she was commissioned in 1990, came up-river to moor alongside HMS *Belfast* on 9 June 2016 for HRH Princess Anne to come on-board and toast the ship farewell. An airport had at last been completed on the island, which would eventually displace the mail service; however, at that time the airport was yet to be commissioned due to severe cross winds, and the British-registered *St Helena* was scheduled to complete several more round trips between Cape Town and St Helena.

The mail ship *St Helena* alongside HMS *Belfast* on 10 June 2016 on a farewell visit, her service to be displaced by a new airport at St Helena on the South Atlantic.

Visiting cruise ships to the Pool moor alongside HMS *Belfast* on a regular basis throughout the summer months. While the larger ships tend to proceed no further than the royals, the smaller vessels come right up to the Pool, providing an attraction for visitors and allowing cruise passengers direct access to the city. Of the many ships, the *Hebridean Spirit* was notable as one of the few British cruise ships to visit the Pool. The largest cruise ship to enter the Pool is the *Minerva II*, owned by Swan Hellenic, coming through Tower Bridge for her naming ceremony on 4 July 2003. She was commissioned in 2001 as *R Eight* for Renaissance Cruises.

During 2016, a typical year for cruise ship visits to the Upper Pool, the season started with the visit of *L'Austral* at the end of April. She was followed in May by the *NG Explorer* and *Minerva*, and in June by *MS Berlin* and twice by *Silver Wind*. The *Silver Wind* came again in July and again in August, followed by *Ocean Majesty* and a return visit by *MS Berlin* – the latter pair revisiting in September. The *NE Brazil, MS Hamburg,* and the *Albatross* visited in September and the final call of the season was made by the *NE Brazil* in October. The ships all tied up alongside HMS *Belfast,* with passengers taken ashore by tender. At George's Stair Tier, just below Tower Bridge, and capable of accommodating vessels up to 110 m in length, were the *NG Orion* and *Kismet,* both in September.

Military visitors are now generally hosted alongside HMS *Belfast*. One of the most recent foreign naval visits was that of the Brazilian training ship *Brasil,* which came alongside the museum ship in June 2016.

Other forms of business promotion have taken place over the years; perhaps one of the nicest was the day the floating gin palace arrived, as E. C. B. Thornton explained in his book *Thames Coast Pleasure Steamers*:

...W A Gilbey, the gin people, chartered the sole remaining Portsmouth and Ryde paddle steamer *Ryde* as a 'floating gin palace' for dour days and moored her off Tower Pier in September 1968. For the occasion her funnel received the large cream, white and red diamond-shaped Gilbey emblem. She did not carry out any cruises.

The cruise ship *Hebridean Spirit* (1991) in the Lower Pool approaching Tower Bridge stern-first, ready to moor alongside HMS *Belfast* on 20 June 2003. [Author]

The *Belfast* hosting the courtesy visit of the Brazilian training vessel *Brasil* (1983) on 15 September 2016. [Author]

Chapter 10

Excursion Ships – Escape to the Coast

In the nineteenth and early twentieth centuries Londoners clamoured for a day out in fresh air away from their grimy city. In the early days the wooden-hulled paddle steamship was quickly recognised as the means to a cheap and affordable day at the seaside. The seaside later became hugely fashionable and the city dwellers were convinced of the health-giving properties of a stiff ozone-filled breeze and even a dip in the sea. Although the prospect of a day out of town sailing down the river was ever appealing to Londoners, the condition of the river above Gravesend was not in the least pleasant. Each house in London had its own cess pit below the ground floor which would periodically be emptied or would more likely overflow into gullies that eventually flowed down to the Thames. Three separate cholera outbreaks claimed several thousand lives over the years until matters finally came to a head in the summer of 1858 when 'The Great Stink' occurred and thousands fled the city. Parliament was obliged to remain in session, hiding behind drapes soaked in chloride of lime at the windows. Joseph Bazalgette was then commissioned to engineer and develop the London sewage system complete with his famous aqueduct to discharge the sewage to the river below Woolwich. In the meantime the prospect of a day trip to Margate or even Gravesend and its amusement park was ever appealing.

With the obvious success of the steamer, a succession of new companies was created to cater for the ever expanding demand for the Thames services; the numerous single ship operators now disappeared very rapidly. Overcrowding was the order of the day; the captains did nothing very much to relieve the situation and collected the fares and encouraged more and more passengers on board. Eventually, some of the companies began employing pursers to collect the fares, and the captains objected to this seeing that their incomes were in danger. As a consequence they gathered together and formed the Sons of the Thames Company.

The Gravesend Steam Packet Company remained the oldest of the established packet companies on the river, along with the Diamond Steam Packet Company and its distinctive black and white diamond patterned funnels. The Diamond, Star and Woolwich companies all competed for the Gravesend trade, the 'Long Ferry'. The Woolwich boats had the reputation of being the dirtiest packets on the river at one time! They started at Charing Cross (Hungerford Market) and called at Greenwich and Queenhithe initially with only two sailings a day to Gravesend. However, the dirty boats of the river were obviously very successful. They also offered the cheapest fares, and rapid fleet expansion prompted services to be developed further afield to Sheerness and Southend. The company had absorbed the Milton & Gravesend Steam Packet Company as early as 1835 with their four steamers, the *Kent, Essex, Pearl,* and *Fly,* which were integrated into its own down-river services.

The success of the Woolwich company antagonised the Watermen's Association. Interference from their members – for example, accidentally leaving barges in the seaway or assisting spillages from flats reportedly caused by the wash of the steamers – was such that intervention was finally called for. The outcome was the formation of the Waterman's Steam Packet Company in 1840. Within four years a fleet of twelve fast and finely appointed steamers operated schedules that just preceded those of the Woolwich company overtly encouraging races to the next pier. The steamers remained popular even when the South Eastern Railway reached Woolwich in 1847, and confidence was not lost in the steamers even when the boiler of the *Cricket* blew up with 150 passengers aboard, killing five of them. The *Cricket* was equipped

The river steamer *Cricket* (1847) 'equipped with a new type of high pressure boiler'. [*The Illustrated London News*]

The wreck of the *Cricket* (1847) 'Steamboat explosion – searching for bodies...' [*The Illustrated London News*]

with a new type 'high pressure' boiler as reported in *The Illustrated London News*, 4 September 1847:

> The *Cricket* had already made two passages between the Adelphi Pier [near Waterloo Bridge] and London Bridge, and was lying off the former landing place at the moment the accident occurred [Friday 27 August 1847].
>
> It appears that the vessel was about to leave the pier for London Bridge, having aboard somewhere about 150 passengers, all quietly seated, when, without the least previous intimation to those on deck, a sudden report was heard, followed by an instantaneous explosion. Immediately the vessel, which had to that moment been filled with persons, was nearly cleared – some of the passengers being actually blown up into the air, falling into the water – others had jumped over the sides, and were struggling in the mud that lined the shore – and but a few, awe-stricken and dumbfounded, remained in the uninjured part of the boat.
>
> The explosion took place in what is usually termed the after part of the vessel... The foredeck remains comparatively uninjured...
>
> One part of the boiler was hurled 100 feet towards the Waterman's Adelphi Pier, at the bottom of George Street, and another portion of it in a contrary direction towards Waterloo Bridge. Exaggerated reports were spread of the number of persons killed. It amounts to five; but a great many were hurt. At least forty or fifty persons were carried upon people's backs, because they were themselves unable to walk...

Fierce and somewhat unhealthy competition ensued for another fifteen years until in 1865 the Watermen's company finally conceded defeat and sold out to the Woolwich Steam Packet Company. In truth, the Watermen's Association, wealthy though it was, refused to put any more resources into its packet company. The 'crack' steamers were imaginatively named *Waterman No. 1, Waterman No.2, Waterman No.3,* and on up to *Waterman No. 12,* while what should have been 13 was given the name *Elphin –* clearly a case of 'unlucky for some'. The Woolwich company subsequently gave the ships bird names such as *Cygnet, Ibis,* and *Osprey,* in the style later adopted for the GSN nomenclature.

The Gravesend Steam Packet Company was reconstituted in 1835 when it employed four ships on the London to Gravesend, Sheerness, Margate and Ramsgate route in competition with GSN. Other competitors were the London & Herne Bay Steam Packet Company with, among other vessels, the popular *Red Rover* and *City of Canterbury.* The *Red Rover* suffered a snapped piston crosshead on passage to London in November 1843, but managed to return to London on one engine, arriving only three hours behind schedule.

On the up-river services, the Iron Steamboat Company and the Citizen Steamboat Company competed for the traffic from the Pool to Chelsea and Kew. The Citizen fleet takes the second prize for least imaginative fleet nomenclature with the series *Citizen A, Citizen B,* up to *Citizen S,* with the exception of the letter 'I'. Subsequent owners, the River Thames Steamboat Company and the Victoria Steamboat Association, tended to give the steamers flower names: A-*Azalea,* C-*Carnation,* D-*Daisy,* F-*Fuschia* etc.

Diamond Packets advertised excursions from London Bridge Wharf to Southend and Sheerness from 1847, calling at the Tunnel, Greenwich, Woolwich, Erith, and Gravesend. They also advertised the *Sons of the Thames* or *Princess Royal* from Hungerford Market Steam Pier (roughly below what is now Charing Cross railway bridge) via London Bridge Wharf to Sheerness, Southend and Chatham.

Cheap railway fares to Gravesend offered by the North Kent Railway and to Southend by the London, Tilbury & Southend Railway put the Star Company, the Thames Company, and the Diamond Steam Packet Company out of business by 1855. At the demise of their owners, the Diamond steamers *Topaz, Ruby, Sapphire,* and *Diamond* were bought by GSN for £4,252.

From 1865 the Woolwich Steam Packet Company was running the steamers *Queen of the Thames* and *Queen of the Orwell* from London Bridge daily to Ipswich. The blockade runner *Alexandra* had been built at Port Glasgow and equipped with state-of-the-art diagonal oscillating engines for agents of the Confederate army, but the American Civil War ended before her completion and in 1865 she was sold to the newly formed Saloon Steam Packet Company, London, for service between London Bridge and Gravesend. She was the first Thames saloon steamer, all previous vessels being flush decked with no deck houses, and was the best appointed and largest steamer on the river at 279 tons gross. Unsurprisingly, she eventually found herself under the colours of the Woolwich Company from the 1875 season onwards.

GSN acquired a number of second-hand steamers in the 1870s, of which the former German passenger tender *Hoboken* was certainly the finest. She became a regular on the husband's boat service to Margate; on Saturdays, a special service called at Tilbury to connect with the train from the city to pick up the husbands that had been working that morning. At Margate the men joined their families at the seaside for the remainder of the weekend.

All was to change from the evening of Tuesday 3 September 1878. The Woolwich Company's *Princess Alice* left Sheerness with 487 passengers bound for Fresh Wharf in the Pool. She picked up another 250 excursionists at Gravesend and set off up-river with her contented passengers listening to a band playing on deck, cheeks aglow from a day at the seaside. Approaching Tripcock Tree Point near Woolwich she was run into by the big collier *Bywell Castle,* which cut open the paddle steamer's hull just forward of the starboard paddle box, flooding the engine room. Passengers were hurled into the river – men, women and their children – while others vainly jumped into the water to save themselves. The total loss was never established, but there was only sixty-nine survivors that evening.

Confidence in the steamers was lost. By 1884 the London Steamboat Company, the main rival to GSN, was effectively bankrupt and most of its assets were purchased by the River Thames Steamboat Company. The popularity of the down-river steamers was never regained as permanent inroads to the trade were made by both the railways and the omnibus.

The year 1885 saw the newly formed River Thames Steamboat Company take over the bankrupt London Steamboat Company, but the new company soon ran out of money as prospective passengers still dwelt on the *Princess Alice* disaster. The River Thames Steamboat Company had received a cash injection of £67,000 from its investors on formation, but as early as June 1886 the whole lot was put up for sale:

> Messrs Fuller, Horsey, Sons & Casell are instructed by the Directors of the River Thames Steamboat Company to offer for sale by tender, as a going concern, in one lot, on Tuesday, 1 June 1886, the business and the whole of the valuable properties of the company comprising: ...The fleet of vessels, consisting of 57 paddle wheel steam vessels adapted for the passenger service of the Thames between London and Hampton Court on the up-river service and below bridge to Greenwich, Woolwich, Gravesend, Sheerness, Southend, Clacton-on-Sea and Harwich. 39 of these vessels have or will have Board of Trade certificates, and include the fast and favourite vessel, the *Glen Rosa* on the Clacton service, the *Alexandra, Albert Edward, Duke of Edinburgh* and *Queen of the Orwell* on the Gravesend, Southend and Sheerness line; and the *Rosalind, Celia* and *Orlando,* built by Sir W Armstrong Mitchell & Co in 1855, and fitted with all recent improvements for light draft navigation; and there are 18 vessels laid up in the docks and yards...

There were no takers and the company was forced to struggle on. The first thing to happen was the cessation of the longer routes to Southend and Clacton-on-Sea, leaving a series of unpaid pier dues in the wake. In 1890, a new injection of cash was identified and the assets and goodwill of the River Thames Steamboat Company became the property of the Victoria Steamboat Association. The excursion fleet was now set to flourish, as the

1890s saw an unprecedented rise in interest in coastal excursions throughout the British Isles; these were very much the halcyon days, *Princess Alice* or not.

The Victoria Steamboat Association was, of course, not alone on the Thames, with the GSN fleet maintaining the lead on the seasonal London to Thanet ports. The decline of the River Thames Steamboat Company in 1886 also allowed two related developments to take place in quick succession; one was an initiative by a business syndicate in Clacton-on-Sea, who wanted to introduce a new company to try and recover the steamer trade to their town to bring Londoners in to spend their money, and the other was a spate of new orders by GSN in response to rumours that the new operator from Clacton would be equipped with modern, fast, and luxurious ships, and who now, in any event, saw an opportunity to enter the Essex coast trade. GSN was also conscious of increasing competition on its traditional London to Thanet and cross-Channel services and was seeking new trade – what better than a service to the newly built pier at Southend and on to Clacton-on-Sea and Great Yarmouth?

It had taken only a few weeks for the syndicate of local traders and businessmen in Clacton to launch their own company, to be known as The London, Woolwich & Clacton-on-Sea Steamboat Company. An order was placed with J. Scott of Kinghorn in Fife for a smart little steamer with compound machinery. The new steamer was given the obvious name of *Clacton* and was ready for the 1888 season. Based at Old Swan Pier above London Bridge, she commenced her daily routine to Clacton and back. The *Clacton* was hugely successful, although a bit small for the run at only 241 tons gross, so at the end of the season the company decided to sell the *Clacton*, while planning an order for a larger and faster vessel for the 1889 season.

GSN embarked on its own new building programme with orders for five new saloon steamers. These were the famous 'classical bird' class of steamers, the first of which, the *Halcyon*, was delivered in 1887 and the last, the *Philomel*, at a cost that had risen to £13,230, in 1889. The other three ships were given the names *Mavis*, *Oriole*, and *Laverock*. Their service speed was a comfortable 17 knots. The ships took over the Thanet and continental trips from London Bridge, and inaugurated a two-day return to Great Yarmouth, with intermediate calls including Gravesend, Southend, and Clacton.

Delays in building the new vessel for the Clacton syndicate were incurred through difficulties in raising the necessary finance. In the end, an order was placed with William Denny & Company of Dumbarton for £19,000 for the new paddle steamer *Clacton Belle*, so inaugurating the famous Belle nomenclature, and ultimately allowing the cumbersome name of the owning company – the London, Woolwich & Clacton Steamboat Company – to be reduced to just Belle Steamers Limited in 1897. The *Clacton Belle* was a much more substantial ship than the *Clacton*, with a gross tonnage of 458 and a speed of 17 knots derived from compound diagonal engines.

A distinctive feature of the ship was her telescopic funnel, which had an ominous tilt to starboard. A fixed funnel with cowl top replaced this in 1900 when the London base moved to Fresh Wharf, which was below London Bridge. In her early days the *Clacton Belle* carried stay sails for use with a fair wind and to inhibit excessive rolling. She was also equipped with traditional wooden paddle floats, which tended to work free, causing significant delays and consequent annoyance to passengers while they were

Southwold Belle (1900) on her morning departure from Fresh Wharf below London Bridge.

reinstalled. She was a two-class ship, with the saloon slightly better appointed than the fore cabin. Caterers were contracted to the ship and described in a contemporary guide as 'distinctly good'.

In 1893 the largest member of the Clacton fleet, the *London Belle*, was commissioned. She was innovative, being the first Thames paddler to have triple expansion steam engines instead of compound engines. Although the *London Belle* was built with a fixed funnel, the foremast was hinged to allow her to berth at Fresh Wharf, with the fore part of the ship lying beneath London Bridge. By the mid-1890s the main Clacton service, operated by the *London Belle*, was advertised to leave Fresh Wharf at 9.30 a.m. daily, calling at Southend Pier at 12.15 p.m. for Clacton. Timings were brought forward slightly in 1900 with advertised connections at Walton for Southwold and Great Yarmouth, as well as Ipswich. The last ship to be built for Belle Steamers was the *Southwold Belle*, which was completed in 1900.

The Victoria Steamboat Association (VSA), as the successor to the River Thames Steamboat Company, bought the famous Clyde steamer *Lord of the Isles* from the Glasgow & Inverary Steamboat Company. She was placed on service on the Thames based at Old Swan Pier in the spring of 1891. The *Lord of the Isles* caused a sensation, being large, fast and comfortable. So impressed were the Directors of the VSA with Inverary Company's funnel colours that they remained unchanged and thereafter were adopted by the VSA – red and black top with two white bands and a central white band near the top of the red section.

Armed with the obvious success of the *Lord of the Isles*, the VSA suddenly found itself being canvassed by the Govan-based Fairfield Shipbuilding & Engineering Company to manage two brand-new crack steamers, to be paid for on long-term

Royal Sovereign (1893) with funnels lowered to pass beneath London Bridge, sailing down the Upper Pool after leaving her berth at Charing Cross.

instalments. The *Koh-I-Noor* was delivered to the VSA in 1892, and the *Royal Sovereign* was delivered to a financially separate company, the London & East Coast Express Steamship Service, in 1893, but was managed by the VSA. In addition, the magnificent steamer *La Marguerite* followed in 1894 under another holding company, Palace Steamers. The ships had bow rudders set into the stem to facilitate steerage while going astern – a particularly useful feature whenever leaving Old Swan Pier above London Bridge. Together, these ships made the GSN fleet, and even the Belle steamers, look very plainly furnished and second-rate.

Each ship was effectively mortgaged from the shipbuilder. The *Koh-I-Noor*, for example, had been built at a cost of £50,900. This was a lot of money in those far-off days, and contrasts with the contract price of £35,360 for her rival, the *London Belle*, reflecting the sumptuous décor and style of completion adopted for the Fairfield/VSA ship. However, despite being a huge success as trendsetters on the Thames, the VSA found it was unable to keep up the payments on the vessels and Fairfield foreclosed the mortgages in 1894. Fairfield then established a new operating company for the fleet under the name New Palace Steamers.

GSN commissioned the new steamer *Eagle* in 1898, conscious that competition was increasing and that the passengers preferred comfort and speed. Although the growth years of the Thames excursion steamer fleets were now finished, the great days were still to come. Overcapacity was good for the traveller, who now had an unprecedented variety and choice coupled with low and competitive fares. The 1890s may have been the boom years for the excursion companies, but the 1900s were set to be those of the excursionist. H. Collard Stone wrote in an article, which first appeared in *Paddle Wheels*, May 1970:

> The steamers catered for the holiday traffic in a big way; as at holiday times the piers often resembled railway stations; but instead of seeing the modern travelling case of today, cumbersome trunks, valises and a whole paraphernalia of baggage went aboard, having to come off again the other end. At Margate and Ramsgate on the arrival and departure of the steamers, dozens of porters, dressed in smocks, with long barrows trundled the baggage to horse drawn cabs waiting at the pier entrance, or vice versa. Even with all this, the steamers were emptied and reloaded in less than ten minutes and away, the next following into the berth in its turn.

GSN's next new steamer for the Fresh Wharf to Southend, Margate and Ramsgate service was the famous paddle steamer *Golden Eagle*. She was a welcome addition, which put GSN back into popularity with the passengers.

Throughout the 1900s, the 'Husband's Boat' continued to serve on Saturdays, the husbands only being able to join their families' seaside weekend after work. The Tilbury-based paddle steamer *Koh-I-Noor* and GSN's fast turbine steamer *Kingfisher* returned to Tilbury with connecting trains from Fenchurch Street, sailing direct to Margate. The *Southwold Belle* took the only London to Margate (via Tilbury) Husband's Boat service, leaving Fresh Wharf at 2 p.m. The rail and sea journeys were interchangeable on the *Southwold Belle*, the return fare being 6s in the saloon and 5s in the fore cabin.

During the First World War the *Golden Eagle* was initially deployed as a troop transport on the English Channel and later she was converted for use as a seaplane carrier. Many of the smaller paddle steamers were commissioned as minesweepers – a role in which they greatly excelled.

The *Clacton Belle* (1890) as the minesweeper HMPMS *930* during the First World War.

All of the Thames excursion steamers survived the war. However, in 1919 the *London Belle* and *Walton Belle* were dispatched to the White Sea via Norway's North Cape as hospital tenders, *HC2* and *HC3*. Here they assisted the expedition against the Bolsheviks in North Russia, supported by the Allies, ostensibly to stem the spread of communism. The pair later returned to the Thames, taking three weeks to complete the journey, before they were finally released by the Admiralty in May 1920.

Both the Coast Development Corporation, owners of Belle Steamers, and New Palace Steamers had gone out of business during the war. They were brought down by arrears in shipbuilders' mortgages at a time when passenger fares were not forthcoming and government charter fees did not cover the outgoings.

Business took a few years to recover in the excursion trade after the war, but by 1922 all but two ships were back in service. The traffic remained seasonal with ships laid up in winter where they were refurbished ready for the new season. In season they were worked hard and their crews worked even harder. Steamers would arrive back at the buoys in the Pool about 10.00 p.m. and open up again at 05.00 a.m. for washing down. During the night period the coal barge would come alongside and a gang of coalies would walk the 25 tons of coal in sacks aboard round the alleyways. The night firemen would clean all fires of clinker and heave it up from the stokehold and dump it in the ash barge. After the coalies had finished, usually about 5.00 a.m., the alleyways, engines, and everything else were all covered with coal dust and the amount of cleaning necessary was enormous.

It was not surprising then that the next new steamer, the *Crested Eagle*, commissioned in 1925, was equipped to burn oil fuel. She took over the Fresh Wharf to Ramsgate service for GSN, displacing the *Eagle* and *Golden Eagle* down-river where they were

Royal Eagle (1932) at the buoys and *Crested Eagle* (1925) leaving the Upper Pool. [DP World]

then based at Greenwich. The *Crested Eagle* had a service speed of over 18 knots and could accommodate 1,650 passengers. Belle Steamers had continued in business despite the bankruptcy of its owners, but ceased to trade after the 1926 season, having been unable to adapt to the depressed trading conditions that prevailed.

Tower Pier was completed in time for the 1929 season and this became the home of most of the excursion paddle steamers. The Pool of London had by then become very congested, and some operators had previously resorted to ferrying their passengers out to the steamers in the river, while others terminated at Greenwich.

GSN was able to face the depression better than most with its numerous coastal and near Continental cargo services, many offering passenger berths as well, providing year-round income. In 1932 GSN commissioned the last of the Thames paddle steamers, the luxuriously appointed *Royal Eagle*. At the same time the New Medway Steam Packet Company took GSN on head-to-head when it introduced the *Queen of Southend* (formerly the *Yarmouth Belle*) to the Pool, sailing to Southend and beyond. The former Mersey Ferry *Royal Daffodil* was acquired for docks cruises from the Pool in the mid-1930s. Southern Railway found that their big turbine steamer *Engadine* was surplus at Dover and deployed her at the Pool between July and August, where she was boarded by tender for cruises down river.

The first big motor ship in the excursion trade was the *Queen of the Channel*, commissioned by the New Medway Steam Packet Company based at Rochester and

The *Royal Eagle* (1932) backing away from Tower Pier in the 1930s. [DP World]

Delightful Afternoon Trips

To GRAVESEND (not landing)

commencing 18th JULY, 1937, on

SUNDAYS, MONDAYS, and TUESDAYS,

during the season, weather and other circumstances permitting, by

S.S. "Royal Daffodil"

LAST SAILING 19th SEPTEMBER.

This Steamer is known the world over as a result of the
important part she played in the famous raid on the
Mole at Zeebrugge in 1918.

Leaving TOWER OF LONDON PIER   2.30 p.m.
„   GREENWICH PIER   -   -   3.00 p.m.

Returning to Tower Pier about 8.30 p.m.

Return Fares:

From Tower Pier 3/-   From Greenwich Pier 2/6

Lunches can be obtained on board from about 1 p.m. at Tower Pier.

Teas and Light Refreshments at popular prices.   Fully Licensed.

Passengers are carried only on the terms and conditions printed on the Company's tickets.

Book at the Pier or in advance from :
GENERAL STEAM NAVIGATION Co., Ltd.,
15, Trinity Square, E.C.3   Tel.: Royal 3200.

BRADLEY & SON, LTD., 115, FLEET STREET, LONDON. E.C.4. AND READING.

'Delightful afternoon trips, commencing 18 July 1937' by the former Mersey Ferry *Royal Daffodil*. (1906)

deployed at Gravesend for day trips to the France and Belgium. She was such a success that a second ship, *Royal Sovereign*, was ordered for delivery in time for the 1937 season. This was a wake-up call for GSN, which promptly bought the Rochester-based company and merged the two operations, placing the *Royal Sovereign* on Tower Pier to Margate,

The *Royal Sovereign* (1937) on a departure from Tower Pier and showing her overhanging lower deck to good advantage.

A poster advertising the services provided by the *Royal Eagle* (1932) from Tower Pier in 1939.

Calais, and Boulogne day trips. She was a big, comfortable ship with accommodation for 1,600 passengers on Thames estuary work and 1,333 on cross-Channel duties. She had an innovative flared-out lower deck that provided additional space for passengers, particularly on the upper deck. The paddle steamer *Royal Eagle*, meanwhile, received an all-white hull down to sponson level in the 1939 season, having even been adorned in shades of biscuit during 1935. These colour schemes were attempts to blend the older steamers with the new image of the motor ships.

One more new motor ship was delivered before the Second World War, the magnificent twin-funnelled *Royal Daffodil*. The *Royal Daffodil* had been ordered in the name of the New Medway Steam Packet Company, although on delivery she was registered under the ownership of GSN. The contract stipulated that she was to be wider than the *Royal Sovereign* in order to reduce rolling, and be able to attain 20¾ knots. She had one-class accommodation for 2,396 passengers and could seat 286 diners in two separate dining rooms. She was delivered on 23 March 1939 at a total cost of £135,660 – just £1,258 over budget. The new ship was an instant, if short-lived, success on the Continental services and no-passport overnight excursions until September, when war once again overtook the nation.

Mr Robert Kelso, Managing Director of GSNC, commented at the launch of the new ship from Denny's yard at Dumbarton on 24 January 1939:

> It is surprising too, how much importance is attached to the number of funnels, especially on a pleasure ship. Most people thought that a ship with two funnels must be twice as good as a ship with one. Originally the *Royal Daffodil* was to be one-funnelled but... two funnels were eventually selected.

Some 20,000 children were evacuated by sea from the capital to reception areas in Felixstowe, Lowestoft and Great Yarmouth over the three days prior to the declaration of war on 3 September 1939, the threat of German air raids being immediate and real. Many more children, of course, were evacuated by rail. The vessels engaged in this work were the *Royal Eagle, Crested Eagle, Golden Eagle, Laguna Belle* (one-time Belle Steamers' *Southend Belle*), *Royal Daffodil, Royal Sovereign, Queen of the Channel,* and *Medway Queen*, a popular paddle steamer employed at Rochester on a service to Southend. The bridge fronts of each vessel were hastily lined in wood cladding and each master was issued with a firearm.

Two former First World War purpose-built paddle minesweepers, converted by the New Medway Steam Packet Company into excursion ships in the 1920s were immediately requisitioned and put back into service as minesweepers. They had served on the Medway and Thames under the names *Queen of Thanet* and *Queen of Kent*. Other ships, including the *Royal Eagle*, were fitted out as anti-aircraft ships. The big motor ship *Royal Sovereign* was requisitioned as HMS *Royal Scot* and used initially between Southampton and Cherbourg, serving the British Expeditionary Force. After that she was taken over for use by the Fleet Air Arm for target practice and she then went north to the Clyde; almost immediately she was recalled to attend at Dunkirk, carrying 16,000 troops home in nine separate trips, with one further trip to St Malo.

The *Royal Sovereign* (1937) disembarking troops at Cherbourg on 16 September 1939.

She was then expected to serve on the Thames but was sunk by an acoustic mine in the Bristol Channel, with the loss of the chief officer.

The other pioneer motor ship, the *Queen of the Channel*, was lost at Dunkirk, as was the paddle steamer *Crested Eagle*. Six other Thames excursion ships, including HMS *Royal Scot*, survived the evacuation of the British Expeditionary Force from the Dunkirk beaches. The new motor ship *Royal Daffodil* received a bomb, which lodged next to the engine room on the port side, but survived the incident. At the end of the war some of the paddle steamers were not fit for refurbishment and were sold. The big *Royal Daffodil* and the steamers *Golden Eagle*, *Royal Eagle*, *Medway Queen*, *Queen of Kent*, and *Queen of Thanet* were all that remained.

By summer 1947 the excursion services were back to normal, although day trips to France were no longer permitted. The highlight of the 1948 season was the entry into service of the new *Royal Sovereign*, built to replace her namesake lost in the war and designed specifically for the Tower Pier to Ramsgate service. Frank Burtt described the new ship as follows:

...trial speed 20.5 knots, gross tons 1,850, passenger accommodation 1,783. The propelling machinery consists of two sets of twelve cylinder Sulzer engines. The main deck has two dining saloons seating 96 and 140 diners respectively. The promenade deck has a smoke room, there is also a sun lounge 145 feet by 33 feet and a covered observation lounge 40 feet in length. With the exception of the main engines, everything is electrically operated.

The post-war *Crested Eagle* (1938) setting out on a docks cruise.

A new *Crested Eagle* started work at Tower Pier, initially carrying school children to the Royal Victoria Dock system with one public cruise on Saturdays only. She had been built in 1938 as the Scarborough-based passenger vessel *New Royal Lady* – a relatively small motor ship with a licensed passenger capacity of 672 for work on the Thames.

The final purpose-built motor ship was the *Queen of the Channel*, replacing her namesake lost at Dunkirk. The new ship had a certificate for 1,350 passengers and provided all the facilities that her slightly larger sister the *Royal Sovereign* could boast, but with 1 foot (0.3 m) less draft and a slightly lower speed of 19 knots. She was delivered in time for the 1949 summer season. Fleet deployment on the Thames, the paddle steamers *Queen of Thanet* and *Queen of Kent* having been sold, was as follows in 1949:

Royal Daffodil	Gravesend to Southend and Margate and cruise to off Cap Gris Nez;
Queen of the Channel	Ramsgate based cruises;
Royal Sovereign	Tower Pier to Margate direct and sea cruise;
Royal Eagle	Tower Pier to Southend, Margate and Ramsgate;
Golden Eagle	Tower Pier to Southend and Clacton;
Crested Eagle	Tower Pier to London Docks, or Gravesend and Southend with short sea cruise.

In 1950 both the *Golden Eagle* and *Royal Eagle* were laid up and later disposed, of the fleet now trading as Eagle Steamers. In 1954 cruises for passport holders to Boulogne were reintroduced using the *Royal Daffodil*; the need for passports was relaxed in 1955 when identity cards only were required.

Eagle Steamers carried on serving Southend and Clacton or Southend and Margate trips from Tower Pier and Continental day trips from Gravesend until it ceased to trade after the 1966 season. Although still popular, the three big motor ships were becoming expensive units to maintain for the all too brief summer season, even though additional business was attracted by providing works charter trips. A company spokesman described the 1966 season as 'grim'. The seamen's strike had affected party bookings and the weather was bad before the season closed in mid-September. In addition, due to the growth of car and coach traffic to the Continent by other routes, the popularity of the day cross-Channel trips to Boulogne and Calais had waned. The *Royal Daffodil* was sold for scrap, while her younger cohorts found service elsewhere.

Two short seasons were offered in 1966 and 1967 by the *Queen of the South*, a former Clyde-based paddle steamer, which was previously named *Jeannie Deans*. She

The start of an educational day trip – school children boarding *Royal Daffodil* (1939) at Tower Pier in June 1961.

The *Waverley* (1947) boarding passengers alongside the Tower Millennium Pier. [Author]

was dogged with mechanical problems and could not pay her way. P & A Campbell of Bristol put the chartered *Queen of the Isles* on the Thames with scheduled departures from Tower Pier in 1969 and again using their *Devonia* in 1977 – neither was a success. Nowadays the Gravesend-based *Princess Pocahontas* comes up to the Pool on excursion work and the preserved paddle steamer *Waverley* does a short season of late-summer cruises from what is now the newly built Tower Millennium Pier.

Chapter 11

Through Traffic

In addition to the through passage of excursion steamers from above London Bridge, a recurrent theme in the Pool has always been the concept of using the tideway as a thoroughfare for transport of passengers into and out of the city. The Penny Fare Ferry, later the Halfpenny Fare Ferry, was the first company dedicated to cheap passenger transport on the river from Westminster through the Pool to Woolwich, but this service came to grief with the loss of the *Cricket* in 1847 (Chapter 11).

The London & Westminster Steamboat Company ran a fleet of small ships in the London area of the Thames, with most services traversing the Pool. This undertaking was largely in competition with the cheaper Halfpenny Fare Steamers. The London & Westminster ships were all named after flowers – the 'flower boats', with bell-topped funnels that were painted black with a distinctive white band. The *London Pride* had her original 8-foot-diameter fixed float paddle wheels replaced with new feathering floats on an 8-foot-diameter wheel in 1849, increasing her speed from just over 10 knots to 13 knots. Many of this generation of ships, built in the 1840s and 1850s, had long careers with a variety of owners on the Thames, including the Citizen Steamboat Company and the Woolwich Steamboat Company. One of them, the *Lotus*, delivered in 1856, survived until 1909, latterly with the London Steamboat Company, the River Thames Steamboat Company, and finally the Victoria Steamboat Association who gave her the name *Lobelia*.

The London County Council voted in favour of running the London Pier river services themselves after the successors of the London Steamboat Company had withdrawn its loss-making services in 1902. During 1904 and 1905 a large and expensive fleet of thirty nearly identical paddle steamers was constructed for the council at a cost of around £6,000 each by the Thames Ironworks, J. I. Thorneycroft & Company at Woolston, Napier & Miller at Glasgow, and G. Rennie at Greenwich and what bonny little boats they were – compound diagonal engines drove them at 12 knots, and with a gross tonnage of between 116 and 125 tons they could carry 530 passengers. Although the promenade deck was open, there was a large awning aft to protect passengers from the vagaries of the London weather, and there was a comfortable lounge on the lower deck. At last the tideway had become a passenger thoroughfare to complement the

The London County Council paddle steamer *Raleigh* (1905) was one of thirty similar steamers on the river until withdrawal in autumn 1907.

new underground train system in the city and it seemed an ideal solution to some of London's burgeoning transport issues.

Frank Burtt takes up the story in *Steamers of the Thames and Medway*:

> Realising the relief it would give to road traffic congestion, the Council again applied for the necessary powers [having already been turned down in 1902]. These were obtained in 1904 and a service was started on 17 June 1905, between Hammersmith and Greenwich with a fleet of thirty steamboats; HRH The Prince of Wales inaugurating the service on the *King Alfred*. The boats were worked on such a heavy loss that they were taken off in October 1907, and on 15 December 1907, the Council decided to sell the thirty boats and invited tenders for their purchase. The total deficiency for the three years working was £162,499. The London County Council disposed of fourteen boats to a new concern called the City Steamboat Company [at a cost of £393 each] which worked a ten minute service from 1909 until August 1914, when the service stopped for the outbreak of war. The other boats were distributed far and wide.

The Council achieved only two things – the removal of all competition on the river and the cessation of the winter service from 1909 onwards. Its bizarre action did, however, provide a glut of little steamers, some surviving in service until the late 1930s. Norman Cox described the affair in an article which first appeared in *The Illustrated London News*, January 1971:

> So the London County Council stepped in like inexperienced weekend sailors. A heavy handed attitude soon antagonised the smaller companies. Their strong challenge was

supported by a deep pocket. They built 30 steamers to carry 500 passengers in each. They built new piers, and employed Captain Arthur Owen, formerly master of *La Marguerite*, as an advisor. With typical muddled bureaucracy, they then built the London tram system and put their own river service out of business.

During 1940, a new passenger service was reinstated on the river as P. N. Thomas recounts in *British Steam Tugs*. It was not introduced as part of any integrated transport policy, but simply as a means of getting up and down the river and avoiding streets damaged or blocked by bomb damage:

> Friday 13 September was chosen for the opening date for the Westminster to Woolwich passenger boat service, organised by the London Passenger Transport Board, in conjunction with the Ministry of Transport, the Port of London Authority and other bodies concerned. Since the London County Council had decided thirty years previously to dispose of its fleet of passenger steamers, there had been no municipal service on the river. At its start the service was run by a number of Mears steamers, the 40 foot motor launch *Jeff* and two motor tugs, *Breezy* and *Gnat*. The tugs were not adapted for passenger carrying and their use was entirely an emergency measure. The *Breezy* covered the 6.7 miles from Westminster Pier to Greenwich Pier in 50 minutes, making four calls on the way. The *Gnat* took half an hour to travel from Greenwich to Woolwich, a distance of 5 miles with one stop.

In 1946 the Thames Waterbus service was introduced, consolidating the wartime interest in the tideway as a means of commuter transport. The new service provided a regular service between Putney and Greenwich, calling at Cadogan, Lambeth, Charing Cross, Tower, Cherry Garden, Wapping, and Limehouse. It was inaugurated using a series of smart diesel vessels such as the *Festival*, some 85 feet in length and carrying up to 250 passengers. In addition, some of the former up-river steamers, such as the *Hurlingham* and *Marchioness*, were also used on the service. R. G. Odell was a major stakeholder in the project, which proved a great success during the war years. The service did survive for a number of years after the war but it was not carried out with any degree of enthusiasm by the respective stakeholders. Indeed, it was eventually overtaken by the modern day tourist boats and bateaux mooches bent on securing the tourists' dollars, rather than chasing the commuters' pounds.

R. G. Odell was not new to river passenger transport and had managed the *New Dagenham* for its subsidiary company Odelia Cruising Motor Ship Company between 1933 and 1937. The role of the *New Dagenham* was a commuter service from Westminster Pier to the Ford Motor Company works at Dagenham – an easy and simple line of direct communication for employees and company visitors between the works and the City. She was a handsome little ship, which had been built in Holland in 1933 especially for the Thames service. Her propulsion units comprised a pair of diesel engines each developing 200 brake horsepower – innovative and cost effective for the route.

The concept of the tideway being used as part of an integrated transport policy finally came about in the early years of the twenty-first century. The most obvious through

The *Neptune Clipper* (2015) in the Upper Pool with Hayes Galleria beyond. [Author]

traffic in the Pool nowadays are the commuter catamarans operated by MBNA Thames Clippers. These provide connecting services with trains and buses and allow use of the pre-paid cut-price London transport Oyster Card on the boats. MBNA Thames Clippers has a fleet of fifteen modern and fast catamarans on the river operating a 50 minute express schedule, 60 minute stopping service, between Putney and Canary Wharf, and from Embankment to Woolwich also in 60 minutes. The catamarans were built in Australia – the present home of fast harbour craft technology – and can operate at speeds greater than 30 knots. MBNA Thames Clippers was founded in 1999 based on a business plan to provide fast commuter traffic on the Thames; the concept proved appropriate for the time and the company prospered until it was taken over in 2006 by the owners of the O2 entertainment complex. They promptly invested in six new catamarans to ensure the development of the company. The newest pair are the *Galaxy Clipper* and *Neptune Clipper,* which were delivered in October 2015 from their builders in Tasmania, having been shipped to the Thames aboard a special heavy lift carrier. The pair cost £6 million to build.

Trip boat operators on the river include City Cruises, Bateaux London, Thames River Services and others. While most of the boats in service are modern, a couple are much older and of historic interest; nevertheless, the safety of all these services is unquestionably high and is a priority for all the operators. This stems partly from the sinking of the trip boat *Marchioness* (used previously on the Thames Waterbus service) on 20 August 1989 when fifty-one party goers lost their lives when the *Marchioness* was run down and sunk near Canon Street railway bridge by the suction dredger *Bowbelle*. From the impact it is believed that the *Marchioness* was totally immersed in just 30 seconds as she rolled under the dredger; anybody below deck could not easily survive. The *Marchioness* sailed downstream from Charing Cross Pier at 1.15 a.m. on a calm moonlit night. The party atmosphere aboard was happy and carefree with passengers enjoying themselves on

The ill-fated *Marchioness* (1923) loading passengers at Westminster Pier, ready for a routine trip on the river.

both the upper and lower decks. The sand dredger *Bowbelle*, meanwhile, had earlier left Nine Elms, also travelling down-river, to load sand at the Shipwash dredging grounds on the lower Thames. As the dredger approached Cannon Street railway bridge she struck the *Marchioness*, first from behind, and then on the side.

The *Marchioness* was one of the older trip boats on the river and had been built at Oxford in 1923, and even attended at the Dunkirk evacuation of the British Expeditionary Force in 1940. Her original steam engine was replaced by a diesel engine in 1950 and she had a covered upper deck added in the 1970s. Following the tragedy, the regulations regarding river passenger boasts were reviewed and increased safety measures adopted. These included limits on alcohol consumption of crew taking charge of a vessel. In addition, in 2002 the Royal National Lifeboat Institution set up four lifeboat stations on the river (there were none before that); one at Gravesend, one at Tower Pier, one at Chiswick Pier, and one up-river at Teddington. They are now the busiest lifeboat stations in the Royal National Lifeboat Institution network.

The main cause of the *Marchioness* tragedy, it would seem, was poor visibility from the steering position on the sand dredger because of the dredging equipment mounted amidships. This is an appalling indictment of small working craft design at that time, and a key factor in the loss of so many young and promising lives. Subsequent investigation also found the instructions to the forward lookout on the *Bowbelle* were inadequate and that the master of the *Bowbelle* should have immediately called for help and lowered his two lifeboats and a rescue craft to help those in the water – he did neither, and it was left to the master of a passing boat, the *Hurlingham* – ironically the near sister of the *Marchioness* – to call for help. Although the master of the *Bowbelle* admitted drinking alcohol during the previous afternoon, this fact was not brought to bear on the outcome of the investigation, the subsequent trials, or at a later enquiry, and the master was allowed to keep his certificate. The master of the *Marchioness*, Stephen Faldo, was drowned along with many of his passengers, only eighty of whom survived.

A number of attempts at through passenger excursion type services have been made over the years, but none with any degree of success. In 1965, for example, the *Darthula II* – one-time Loch Etive excursion boat – was scheduled to run from Erith to Tower Pier and on to Kew and Richmond. With a capacity of 120 passengers she was hard ship to fill on the up-river cruise, despite the obvious attractions of such a trip, and only lasted one season. Competition that year came from the Tilbury to Gravesend ferry, which, on Wednesdays and Sundays, took a cruise up to Tower Pier via Greenwich. This service was normally taken by the *Edith*.

Through cargo services, the so called 'up-river' steamer, have long been a feature of the Pool. Tugs with hinged funnels to negotiate the numerous fixed bridges took barges loaded with goods both up and down the river, to and from the docks and the busy riverside wharves. The barges were loaded and unloaded at numerous small jetties and quaysides along the river, throughout London, and above Teddington, servicing the numerous riverside factories and warehouses. A most important up-river commodity was coal, brought into the Thames by collier from both north-east England and South Wales. The trade had been carried on since the nineteenth century when coal first began to be used as a fuel in London alongside the traditional domestic fuel of timber. The main consumers of coal in the nineteenth and twentieth century, however, were the gas generating plants and, at a later stage, the riverside electricity power stations.

Coal gas was extracted from coal in a special process that released the gas for domestic consumption, and left a clean fuel called coke for industrial use. Ridley Chesterton and Fenton describe the early days of the industry:

> The coal needs of the infant gas industry were at first met by the huge fleet of sailing colliers which ponderously and – in times of bad weather – uncertainly brought most of London's supplies from the collieries of Northumberland and Durham. But the steamship was evolving, becoming gradually more practical and well-accepted, and in the 1850s it was given a major fillip by the Gas, Light and Coke Company which took two screw colliers on charter. The experiment was a great success: the company was supplied with coal more cheaply and more reliably, and in future most major gas works were built where steamships could berth alongside. And the steam collier never looked back.

The problem arose when gas plants started to be built in west London. Conventional steam colliers were forbidden access to these by the low air draft of London Bridge and other fixed bridges that were constructed up-river. One of the first of the up-river gas works was at Nine Elms and in 1878 two innovative low air draft colliers were specially designed to negotiate the Thames bridges and bring coal directly to the plant without the need to tranship the cargo into barges. These were the first of the Thames 'flat-irons', named *Westminster* and *Vauxhall*, owned by a small ship owner,

The up-river collier *Joseph Swan* (1938), photographed on her acceptance trials and belonging to the London Power Company, was one of many such ships lost in the Second World War; torpedoed in the North Sea in September 1940, only one of her crew of eighteen men survived.

Escomb & Howard of London, and immediately chartered for use on the run from north-east England down the North Sea coast and up the Thames to central London to discharge at Nine Elms.

The first true flat-iron was the *Wandle,* delivered to the Wandsworth & Putney Gas Light and Coke Company. She was designed to deliver coal to its works at Wandsworth, sixteen bridges up from Tower Bridge. She was soon joined by a slightly larger sister, which was christened the *Mitcham.* This pair proved the concept of up-river, low air draft, sea-going colliers and, thereafter, all the gas and electricity generating stations above the Pool were supplied directly by this type of ship. Craig J. M. Carter wrote in *Sea Breezes,* February 1958:

> The passage of the up-river ships to berths at Nine Elms or Fulham was, and still is, a particularly tortuous one, involving the careful navigation of the crowded tideway, and its many bends, and the negotiation of some 16 low-span bridges. It will be readily understood that the deck erections of any vessel intended for up-river work must be limited to the navigable height of what are termed the 'working arches' of certain key bridges, and that the conditions entail the most careful treatment of design in relation to draft, ballasting, overhead clearances and navigation in general. Hence the unusual appearance of the 'flattie', and although the modern vessels of today have become rather more streamlined, it is not possible, by any stretch of imagination, to describe the first ships of this type as good-looking craft.

The North Sea collier convoys were particularly badly hit during the Second World War and all the collier fleets suffered significant losses. As a consequence, a post-war rebuilding programme was carried out and numerous flat irons were built between 1949 and 1958 for what had then become the South Eastern Gas Board, the North Thames Gas Board,

The *Croydon* (1951) was typical of the post-war up-river 'flat-irons' that supplied coal to the power stations and coking plants above London Bridge. [Author]

The last of the flat-iron colliers, the *Lambeth* (1958) coming down-river in the Upper Pool. She was the final ship to be completed in a group of five identical ships built for the South Eastern Gas Board.

the North Eastern Gas Board, and the nationalised Electricity Generating Authority. Typical of the post-war ships was the *Croydon*, commissioned in 1951 by the South Eastern Gas Board. During the late 1960s, natural gas from the North Sea was available and coal gas generation was phased out. At the same time the power generating plants in London were closed as larger generating capacity came online to supply the National Grid. Consequently, the traditional Thames collier fleets were extinct by 1971 and coal no longer passed through the Pool. Oil fuel shipments, however, continue to this day.

Through traffic also included large quantities of compressed domestic and commercial waste. This was loaded into specially constructed barges up-river at Grosvenor Dock above Chelsea Bridge, which were towed down through the Pool to Rainham in Essex where there were large disposal facilities to landfill. The transfer involved over 1 million tons of rubbish each year, all passing through the Pool. The waste transfer by barge ceased in 1995 and the traffic was transferred to road transport, while recycling of waste was introduced instead of simple disposal to landfill.

Just very occasionally the visitor to the Pool will see one of the static use vessels moored alongside the Victoria Embankment on its way to or from periodic dry docking. These ships tend to have hinged masts and funnels to negotiate London Bridge. Modern paint preparations mean that they only need to be out of the water once every ten years or so while other maintenance is carried out *in situ*. Among the favourites was the former Clyde turbine steamer *Queen Mary*, which left the Embankment for lay-up at Tilbury in 2009 and is now under restoration on the Clyde.

The *Conformity* (1940) was a small tanker owned by F. T. Everard & Sons, seen approaching Tower Bridge in the Lower Pool in January 1969 with fuel oil for up-river installations. [Author]

The former Clyde passenger steamer *Queen Mary* (1933) was moored alongside the Embankment between 1997 and 2009, and was one of a number of otherwise static ships needing to pass through the Pool for periodic dry docking. [Author]

Chapter 12

Artefacts and Landmarks

London Bridge, Tower Bridge, indeed the Tower of London, and many of the old docks remain as they were, now a memorial to the original Port of London. Tower Bridge is a special landmark as it evokes the hustle and bustle of the river when the Upper Pool was in its heyday in the years leading up to the 1960s. The bascules opened and closed for the sea-going traffic on a regular schedule. The morning excursion departures from Tower Pier were especially irksome to commuters into the city, many of whom sought alternative means of getting across the river to their office desks during the summer season.

Henry Major Tomlinson (1873-1958), a sensitive and perceptive commentator of his time, noticed 'that the multitude who cross London Bridge every day' preferred the east side of the bridge – the one overlooking the Pool. Once there, they could not 'resist a pause to stare overside' at 'another life below, with its strange cries and mysterious movements'. For Tomlinson, a ship departing through Tower Bridge evoked thoughts of a 'world beyond the one we know'. The spell ended only with the lowering of Tower Bridge, when 'the gates to the outer world close again'. This perception remains true to this day.

Many of the wharves remain much as they used to be, only now the quaysides remain silent; the cranes and other equipment have gone and the dockers' banter is now a thing of the past. The wharf warehouses were sturdily built with floors strengthened to carry heavy loads. Rather than demolish these fine buildings following the decline of the Pool as a port in the early 1970s, many have been converted for domestic and commercial use. For the most part these changes have been carried out in keeping with the flavour of the riverside scene, while St Katherine Dock and other smaller docks have been modified for use as marinas for private boats, along with attractively modified warehouse blocks now converted into domestic and retail properties.

Archaeological artefacts are numerous and recent finds show light on the shipbuilding activity that the Thames once hosted. The supremacy of the Thames for shipbuilding was a reflection of the pride of the merchants of London in their port and their ships. This continued until the 1850s but shipbuilding then declined rapidly as other centres adopted the construction of the iron hull and the steam engine. The decline on the Thames was exacerbated by the rigid system of wage contracts, strong labour unions, high wages and overheads, plus the distance from the iron and coal resources. The main surviving shipbuilder thereafter was the Thames Ironworks – one time Ditchburn & Mare – at Blackwall.

Shipbuilding in the Pool, notably at Bellamy's Wharf at Rotherhithe, had, nevertheless, once been an important activity, as David Saxby and Damian Goodburn describe in *The Mariner's Mirror*, Part 2, 1998:

> During the seventeenth century Rotherhithe, or 'Redriff,' developed as a settlement of shipbuilders, timber and hemp merchants, mastmakers, caulkers, potters and others located along the shore of the Thames. A number of well-known shipbuilders included William Castle, Jonas Shish and Sir Anthony Deane. Sir William Warren's timber yard was also located at Rotherhithe.
>
> ...archaeological excavation at Bellamy's Wharf [Rotherhithe] has provided a rare opportunity to examine details of ship and dock construction during the seventeenth century and of shipbuilding and shipbreaking activities during the eighteenth and nineteenth centuries. From the documentary sources and archaeological evidence it seems likely that the dock was built by the shipbreaker and timber merchant Thomas Gould between 1660 and 1670. The names of the parent vessels from which the timbers derive are hard to ascertain, though it is possible that the timbers from the first phase of dock construction represent either ships sold by the Navy around 1660 or a vessel already owned by the Gould family, perhaps the *Morning Star*, *Crow* or the *Heartsease*. The ship timbers used to rebuild the dock are likely to have come from at least two ships broken up by Thomas Gould around 1667-70, possibly from the Dutch raid on the Medway in June 1667. These vessels would have provided a convenient source of timber for reuse in dock building.

One other interesting artefact is Cleopatra's Needle situated on the Embankment – a priceless Egyptian column dating back some 3,500 years. It was made in Egypt for the Pharaoh Thotmes III in 1460 BC. It is known as Cleopatra's Needle only because it was brought from Alexandria, the royal city of Cleopatra, to commemorate the British victory over Napoleon, sixty-three years earlier. The column had actually been presented to Britain sixty years earlier.

A specially-designed cigar-shaped boat, the *Cleopatra*, was used to ship the obelisk to the UK in 1877. The *Cleopatra* was designed and built by the Thames Ironworks and assembled in Alexandria around the obelisk, with the fore and aft peaks secured with a concrete seal to create an iron cylinder some 93 feet long. A cabin, bilge keels, bridge and rudder were fitted and she set off from Alexandria in company with the steamship *Olga*. The *Olga* lost her tow and five of her crew during a storm. A contemporary one penny pamphlet described what happened next:

> [The *Cleopatra*] was picked up by the English steamer *Fitzmaurice* near the spot where the *Olga* had left her, and was towed into Ferrol on the coast of Spain, where

a lien on her was placed for salvage by the captain of the *Fitzmaurice*. After many weeks detention her salvage was settled for [£2,000], and she was taken 'out of pawn' by the *Anglia* sent from England, and was safely towed without any further mishap from Ferrol Bay to the Thames, and finally moored in the East India Docks in the first month of 1878. The needle's last venture on the water before her erection on the ground chosen for her in her new home took place at an early hour of the morning of Saturday February 2nd. The arrangements for unlocking the *Cleopatra* were then made under the supervision of Colonel Du Plat Taylor, Secretary of the East India Dock Company, Mr Astat, Superintendent, and Captain Marrable, Dock Master. After being towed into the river by the *Era*, ...the *Trogan* and another tug were firmly lashed on either side of the *Cleopatra* to make her steer steadier than she did on the previous voyage, and were handsomely dressed with the flags of the Shipwrights' Company, commanded by Mr Lovell, the pilot, in company with Captain Carter, who brought the *Cleopatra* from Alexandria. The public excitement became so intense that those who could afford the expense chartered several wherries all along the Thames to get a close inspection. Accompanying Mr Dixon (who was responsible for the work of bringing the needle to England) and friends, were Sir Charles Adderley, President of the Board of Trade. An escort was provided by the Thames Conservancy Board's Launch, in charge of Captain James, having on board Admiral Ommaney and some other members, who went ahead to secure a clear course for the procession. Captain Carter with his mate, Mr Matthews, and the same crew as brought her over, were on board. Guns were fired from several wharfs in response to which she saluted; and besides multitudes on both the river banks, crowds hailed from all the bridges although so early in the morning.

HMS *Belfast* departing Devonport towards the end of her active career. [*Western Morning News*]

One obvious newcomer now dominates the Upper Pool, the former light cruiser HMS *Belfast*. Construction of *Belfast* – the first Royal Navy ship to be named after the capital city of Northern Ireland, and one of ten Town-class cruisers – began in December 1936 and she was commissioned in August 1939 shortly before the outbreak of the Second World War. Her first duties were the British naval blockade against Germany, but in November the *Belfast* struck a German mine and spent the next two years undergoing extensive repairs, where she was also equipped with improved firepower, radar equipment, and armour. *Belfast* saw action escorting Arctic convoys to the Soviet Union during 1943, and in December 1943 played an important role in the Battle of North Cape. In June 1944 *Belfast* took part in Operation Overlord supporting the Normandy Landings, firing shells over the Allied troops at German positions above the beachheads. In June 1945 *Belfast* was redeployed to the Far East to join the British Pacific Fleet, arriving shortly before the end of the Second World War. *Belfast* saw further combat action in 1950–52 during the Korean War and then underwent an extensive modernisation programme between 1956 and 1959. However, it was not long before *Belfast* entered the reserve in 1963.

In 1967, efforts were initiated to preserve Belfast as a museum ship. A joint committee of the Imperial War Museum, the National Maritime Museum, and the Ministry of Defence was established, and reported in June 1968 that the structure of the vessel was sound and that preservation was possible. In 1971 the HMS Belfast Trust began to campaign for her preservation and the government transferred the ship to the trust in July 1971. She was then brought up to the Pool to specially constructed moorings off what was once Hays Wharf. Opened to the public in October 1971, *Belfast* became a branch of the Imperial War Museum in 1978; she is now a popular tourist attraction, with over a quarter of a million visitors each year.

The museum ship *Belfast* is a pertinent reminder of Britain's maritime history and the nation's fight for supremacy on the seas. Although a contrast to the local port history of the Pool itself, it is appropriate that *Belfast* is moored in the Upper Pool as a focal point for a reach of the river that is now devoid of commercial activity. As such the *Belfast* adds value to the diverse landmarks and artefacts of both the Upper and Lower Pools, the nucleus of the Port of London, which was once rich in activity, and the driver of the city's wealth.

Currently lying in the Docklands, secure on a floating pontoon, is a wonderful artefact of the Thames and its former shipbuilding industry. This is the steam coaster *Robin*, which was built in 1890 by McKenzie, MacAlpine & Company, Orchard House Yard, Blackwell, on the site of the former Thames Ironworks. She was ordered by owners in South Wales, but most of her long working career was spent under the Spanish flag. In 1974 she was rescued from the scrapyard and brought back to Rochester to be renovated and from there she adopted an exhibition role in St Katherine Dock, but in 1991 she was displaced to the West India Dock and has since received much love and well-deserved attention to ensure that this important artefact remains in posterity. She now lies securely on her pontoon in the Royal Victoria Dock, near the end of the City Airport runway.

The paddle steamer *Princess Elizabeth* was berthed at St Katherine Pier in 1970 and three years later moved alongside Old Swan Pier above London Bridge until 1978 where, during her stay, she was used as a restaurant. She is a former Isle of Wight ferry and made four voyages to the beaches at Dunkirk to help in the evacuation of the British Expeditionary Force in 1940; it is fitting that she now lies as a museum ship in Dunkirk harbour, looking resplendent in her red and black livery from her Isle of Wight days.

The steam coaster *Robin* (1890) as she appeared when she took up station in St Katherine Dock as a museum ship. She now lies preserved on a floating pontoon in the Royal Victoria Dock.

The preserved wartime standard puffer type coaster *VIC 196* (1945) seen off Butlers Wharf on a trip up from her current home at Chatham.

A number of other historic vessels and replicas are berthed in the Docklands. Several Thames and Continental barges are preserved in St Katherine Dock, some providing short cruise opportunities from time to time. St Katherine Dock itself is now a marina and developed with an array of domestic and retail properties, making it an attractive reminder of the busy working dock it once was. The same is the case at London Dock and at Shadwell Basin. Elsewhere, the numerous riverside wharves have either been converted for domestic or commercial use, or demolished and replaced by new buildings as part of the Docklands redevelopment programme. All serve as wonderful reminders of the working port. Then, of course, there is Tower Bridge, which still raises its bascules as required for passing traffic. This includes the numerous visitors to the Pool, which lie alongside HMS *Belfast,* as well as the regular visits by some of the sailing barges and other occasional visitors.

All this is a far cry from the Pool 100 years ago, with its thriving port industries and numerous ships queuing up at the mid-river buoys awaiting a berth. One little group of small paddle steamers from the past sum up other changes that have occurred in this time – changes in the social and the human foci of society: the fleet of the managers of the Metropolitan Asylum District. The steamers with their black funnels with a single brown band were the *Albert Victor* and *Marguerite*, both built in 1879, the *Maltese Cross* and

The preserved Thames Barge *Cabby* (1928) – the last of the wooden Thames sailing barges to be built – lying at the London Bridge City Pier in the Upper Pool in June 2001.

Geneva Cross, both built in 1894, and the *Red Cross,* dating from 1901. All except the *Red Cross* were built in London. The role of these little ships? They were used to take patients with suspected infectious diseases from the clearing house at Rotherhithe down-river to the city's isolation hospital – an old battleship, a redundant frigate, and the obsolescent twin-hulled cross-Channel ship *Castalia* – all lying in Long Reach off Dartford.

It would seem that society has moved forward these past hundred years. While we lost the port activity in the Pool, we gained in other ways. The Pool, itself an artefact, is not a museum of the port that once was, but rather a reminder of that industry. The river through the Pool, Upper and Lower, is now a busy highway with fast and modern passenger commuter services operating at regular and frequent intervals between Putney and the Docklands. Even the old dock areas of St Katherine, London Dock and Shadwell Basin have been put to good use for new and diverse interests keeping them alive rather than just static, obsolete and unused parts of East London.

The view from either Tower Bridge, or from London Bridge at the head of the Upper Pool, remains as enchanting as ever. The cranes, the ships, the lighters and the tugs might all now have gone, but if you close your eyes and stand on the downstream side of London Bridge and shut out the noise of the traffic, you can still feel the hustle and bustle that once was. Perhaps the Batavier ships setting off for Rotterdam, perhaps the *Baltabor* heading off downstream for the Baltic or even the big Spanish-flagged passenger and cargo ship *Monte Ulia* working cargo alongside New Fresh Wharf. These are the memories of a working port; a port manned and worked by its own people, people who lived near their work in Wapping or Rotherhithe, and people who were the life and soul of the Pool.

The many trip boats and commuter services now available on the Thames allow the visitor to enjoy the river at close quarters from, for example, Westminster Pier through the Upper and Lower Pools, and into the lower reaches of the Thames. It is even possible during the late summer season to take the paddle steamer *Waverley* from the Tower Millennium Pier for a day trip to the seaside. The preserved former Clyde paddle steamer *Waverley* sails through Tower Bridge down-river to destinations such as Southend and Margate, and evokes fond memories of Eagle Steamers 'weather and other circumstances permitting' and their wonderful post-war trio *Royal Daffodil, Royal Sovereign,* and *Queen of the Channel.*

One of the many contemporary trip boats on the river, *Millennium of Peace* (1999), seen from London Bridge with the old Billingsgate Fish Market building and quayside on the left. [Author]

The *Princess Pocahontas* (1962) passing down-river above Tower Bridge on 24 September 2003. [Author]

The *Waverley* (1946) below Tower Bridge on 27 September 2006 with trippers bound for Southend and the Medway. [Author]

The great Tower Bridge still dividing the Upper from the Lower Pool. [Author]

But above all, looking down across the Upper and Lower Pool is the White Tower. This, the oldest of all the artefacts, remains a symbol of the authority of the City of London and of the city's reliance on the trade generated by the Port of London for the global authority that London commands today. At the upstream end of the north bank of the Pool is Adelaide House, the first steel-structured 'skyscraper' in London and the tallest building in the city when it was built in the mid-1920s. The hidden gem among all this is undoubtedly the old Billingsgate Fish Market building, built in 1850 and situated just downstream from Adelaide House. This enchanting building is now used as an events venue. Immediately downstream is the old Custom House building, completed in 1817 and still occupied by Her Majesty's Customs and Excise, although the building is largely screened off from the river by a line of trees. Thus, the Upper and Lower Pools remain a fascinating part of London, steeped in history and a wonderful reminder of the port industry that once came right up into the city itself.

A final and memorable descriptive image of the Pool is that by novelist Emily Brontë, who described the harassing business of hiring a waterman to board ship lying in the river. The account is based on her own experiences travelling to work in a school in Brussels in 1842 and is taken from the novel *Villette*, first published in 1853 (the steamer *Vivid* was a GSN steamer built in 1835 and which was acquired by GSN in 1841, although she normally served between London and Hull):

This was an uncomfortable crisis. It was a dark night. The coachman instantly drove off as soon as he got his fare; the watermen commenced a struggle for me and my trunk. Their oaths I hear at this moment: they shook my philosophy more than did the night, or the isolation, or the strangeness of the scene. One laid hands on my trunk. I looked on and waited quietly; but when another laid hands on me I spoke up, shook off his touch, stepped at once into a boat, desired austerely that the trunk be placed beside me 'just there', which was instantly done; for the owner of the boat I had chosen became now an ally; I was rowed off.

Black was the river as a torrent of ink; lights glanced on it from the piles of buildings round, ships rocked on its bosom. They rowed up to several vessels; I read by lantern light their names painted in great white letters on a dark ground. The *Ocean* and the *Phoenix*, the *Consort*, the *Dolphin*, were passed in turns; but the *Vivid* was my ship, and it seemed she lay further down.

The *Vivid* started out, white and glaring, from the black night at last. 'Here you are' said the waterman, and instantly demanded six shillings...

But there is, of course, one more major living artefact – the legacy of the ships that came to the Pool of London. That legacy is the City itself; without the Pool offering safe haven for ships, yet being shallow and narrow enough to bridge, there would have been no London. The Hanseatic League recognised the strategic importance of both the Pool along with its ships and the City. Trade, marketing, transhipping, and all the other activities of the Pool of London only came about because of the ships that were able to come safely to the Pool to conduct their business. Without them Londinium would have remained just that – Londinium.

Overlooking Shadwell Basin, watching the ships, a photograph taken in 1950.

The Lower Pool in its heyday – GSN's *Nautilus* (1874) and *Lapwing* (1879) beyond at Irongate Wharf. [DP World]

Appendix

The Wharves of the Upper and Lower Pools

SOUTH BANK	NORTH BANK
LONDON BRIDGE	
Fenning's Wharf	London Bridge Wharf
Sun Wharf	Fresh Wharf
Topping's Wharf	Cox and Hammond's Wharf
Chamberlain's Wharf	Nicholson's Wharf
Cottons Wharf	Grant's Quay Wharf
Humphry's Wharf	Billingsgate Market
Hay's Dock and Wharf	Custom House Wharf
Willsons Wharf	Custom House and Wool Quays
Griffin's Wharf	Galley Dock and Quay
South Thames Wharf	Chester Quay
Gun & Shot Wharves	Brewer's Quay
Symon's Wharf	Tower Pier
Stanton's Wharf	
St Olave's Wharf	
Pickle Herring Wharf	
Mark Brown's Wharf	
Tower Bridge Wharf	
TOWER BRIDGE	
Burtt's Portland Wharf	Irongate Wharf
Anchor Brewhouse	St Katherine's Wharf
Butler's Wharf	Harrison's Wharf
Horselydown Wharf	South Devon Wharf

Coventry's Wharf	British & Foreign Wharves
Cole's Wharves	Miller's Wharf
Newell's Wharf	Carron Wharf
Shad Thames	London & Continental Steam
St Saviour's Dock	London Dock
St Andrew's Wharf	Hermitage Steam Wharf
Meriton's Wharf	Colonial Wharves
Reed's Wharf	Standard Wharves
Uveco Wharf	Watson's Wharf
Deverell's Wharf	Black Eagle Wharf
Downing's Wharf	Brewers Wharf
Reed's Lower Wharf	Albion Wharf
Redman's Wharf	Hasties Wharf
Springall's Wharf	St Helen's Wharf
Adlard's Wharf	London Dock
Brunswick Wharf	Oliver's Wharf
Seaborne Coal Wharf	Orient Wharf
London Grist Mills	Gun Wharf
East Lane Wharf	St John's Wharf
Chamber's Wharves	Morocco Wharf
Bond's Wharf	Eagle Sufferance Wharf
Fountain Dock	Eagle Wharf
Darnell's Wharf	Baltic Wharf
Fountain Stairs Wharf	Old Aberdeen Wharf
Powell's Wharf	St John's Wharf
Farrand's Wharf	Sun Wharf
Cherry Garden Wharf	Swan Wharf
Lucas and Spencer's	King Henry's Wharves
Corbett's Wharf	Gibb's Wharf
National Wharf	Gun Wharves
Platform Wharf	Middleton & St Bride's
Platform Sufferance	Foundry Wharf
Braithwaite & Dean's	St Hilda's Wharf
Pace's Wharf	New Crane Wharves
Cochin Wharf	Lower Oliver's Wharf
Yardley's Wharf	Lushes Wharf
Matthew's Wharf	Metropolitan Wharf
Rotherhithe Wharf	Thorpe's and Queen
Cannon Wharf	Pelican Wharf

Abbot's Wharf	Shadwell Basin
Gordon's Wharf	Coal Wharf
Prince's Wharf	Bowle's Wharf
Carr's Wharf	Free Trade Wharf
Beard's Wharf	Hubbuck's Wharf
East India Wharf	Ratcliff Cross Wharf
Bombay Wharf	Lendrum's Wharf
Hope Wharf	Phoenix Wharf
Grice's Wharf	Trinity Ballast Wharf
Claydon's Wharf	Marriage's Wharf
Genisi's Wharf	Roneo Wharf
Brandram's Wharf	London Wharf
Fisher's Sufferance Wharf	Crown Mill Wharf
Cumberland Wharf	Eagle Wharf
Carolina Wharf	New Sun Wharf
Ransome's Wharf	Vanes Wharf
Norway Wharf	Oporto Wharf
Clarence Wharf	Old Sun Wharf
Dinorwic Wharf	Chinnok's Wharf
Surrey Commercial Wharf	Regent's Canal
Bull Head Wharf	Victoria Wharf
King and Queen Wharf	Hough's Wharf
Bellamy's Wharf	Dover Wharf
Prince's Wharf	Blyth Wharf
Lower King & Queen Wharf	Broadway Wharf
Upper Globe Wharf	Etheridge's Wharf
Normandy Wharf	Fielder's Wharf
Crown Lead Works	Lamb's Wharf
Horseferry Wharf	Spark's Wharf
Grand Surrey Wharf	Moline Wharf
Lavender Dock	Duke Shore Wharf
Lavender Lock entrance	Anchor Wharf
Pageant Wharf	Dunbar Wharf
Upper Ordnance Wharf	Limekiln Dock
Sunderland Wharf	
Cuckold's Point	

Bibliography

Auten, Harold, *Q Boat Adventures, the Exploits of the Famous Mystery Ships by a Q Boat Commander* (London: Herbert Jenkins Ltd, 1919)

Bowman, Tracey, *The Story of the Tower of London* (London: Merrell Publishers Ltd, 2015)

Burtt, Frank, *Steamers of the Thames and Medway* (London: Richard Tilling, 1949)

Cope Cornford, L., *A century of sea trading, 1824-1924* (London: A & C Black, 1924)

Greenway, Ambrose, *A Century of North Sea Passenger Steamers* (Shepperton: Ian Allan Ltd, 1986)

Guinness Broodbank, Joseph, *History of the Port of London* (London: Daniel O'Connor, 1921)

Hancock, H. E., *Semper Fidelis, the Saga of the 'Navvies'* (London: General Steam Navigation Co., 1949)

McRonald, Malcolm, *The Irish Boats, Volume 1, Liverpool to Dublin* (Stroud: Tempus Publishing Ltd, 2005)

Morton H. V., *In Search of London* (London: Methuen & Co., 1951)

Moyse-Bartlett H., *A History of the Merchant Navy* (London: George Harrap & Co., 1937)

Ridley Chesterton, Douglas and Roy Fenton, *Gas and Electricity Colliers; The Sea-going Ships Owned by the British Gas and Electricity Industries* (Kendal: World Ship Society, 1984)

Robins, Nick, *Birds of the Sea: 150 Years of the General Steam Navigation Company* (Portishead: Bernard McCall, 2007)

Robins, Nick, *An Illustrated History of Thames Pleasure Steamers* (Great Addington: Silverlink Publishing Ltd, 2009)

Robins, Nick, *Coastal Passenger Liners of the British Isles* (Barnsley: Seaforth Publishing, 2011)

Schneer, Jonathan, *The Thames: England's River* (London: Abacus, 2005)

Thomas P. N., *British Steam Tugs* (Albrighton: Waine Research, 1983)

Thornton, E., *Thames Coast Pleasure Steamers* (Prescot: T. Stephenson & Sons Ltd, 1972)